Bargello Hearts

by Nancy Podolsky

with Debra & Sim Ayers

Mary —
Happy Mother's Day.
Keep on quilting and have
fun making hearts.

Nancy Podolsky
May 1996
Oakdale, CA

DOHENY PUBLICATIONS, INC.
P.O. Box 1175
Edmonds, Washington 98020
(206) 774-3761

Acknowledgments

Many thanks to:
❦ Debra Ayers for bringing the Bargello Heart to my shop. ❦ My husband for supporting my "habit" of fabric. ❦ My three children for putting up with many "nuked" meals. ❦ My Mom for always sewing samples. ❦ My Dad for being such a great "gofer." ❦ Vicki Rapaport, Susan Godkin, Margie White, and Mary Blackford for testing the instructions. Also Rhoda Lonergan and Kathie Koepsell for test sewing. ❦ Launa Peters, Mary Blackford, and my Mom, Norene Michener, for all their proofreading. ❦ All my students and friends who made the quilts photographed for this book. ❦ Doheny Publications for polishing the text and publishing this book.

Dedicated with love to my family,

Nancy Podolsky

Credits

Editing: Diane Roubal, Marilyn Doheny
Copy Editing: Gail Newman
Photography: Mark Frey
Layout Plans: Sim Ayers
Design & Production: Cynthia Peterson

Front Cover Quilt: K.H.K + T.D.K by Kathie Koepsell, 74" x 81".
Back Cover Quilt: Agua Fresca by Laura Podolsky, 62" x 66".

Bargello Hearts
© 1996 by Nancy Podolsky

Doheny Publications
P.O. Box 1175
Edmonds, WA 98020

ISBN 0-945169-17-5

Library of Congress Catalog Card Number: 96-83510

Published 1996
Printed in Hong Kong

Contents

About the Authors 4

1 ❧ Introduction 5
The Bargello Heart Process 6

2 ❧ Supplies 7
Equipment List 7
Choosing a Quilt Size 8
Purchasing the Fabric 8
Batting 9
More About Tools 9
More About Fabric 10

3 ❧ Fabric Selection 11
Fabric Color and Design Choices 12
Arranging the Fabrics 12
Visualizing Your Design 16
Blank Layout Plan 17
Fabric Charts 18

4 ❧ Cutting Fabric Strips 19
Fabric Preparation 19
Cutting Technique 21

5 ❧ Strata Construction 23
Sewing and Pressing 24
Using Directional Fabrics 25
Creating Strata Units 26

6 ❧ Counter-Cuts 27
Preparing the Strata 28
Cutting Technique 28
Counter-Cut Charts 29
Heart Assembly Preview 30

Bargello Heart Gallery 31
A Sample Fabric Arrangement 32

7 ❧ Basic Heart Construction 49
Overview 50
Construction Technique 51
Basic Size — 53" x 60" 52
Basic Size Layout Plan 54

8 ❧ Version 1 Heart Construction 57
Twin Size — 47" x 76" 58
Twin Size Layout Plan 60
Full Size — 53" x 76" 63
Full Size Layout Plan 64
Queen Size — 60" x 80" 67
Queen Size Layout Plan 68

9 ❧ Version 2 Heart Construction 71
Mini Size — 22" x 29½" 72
Mini Size Layout Plan 74
Baby Size — 33" x 55" 76
Baby Size Layout Plan 78
King Size — 80" x 80" 80
King Size Layout Plan 82

10 ❧ Design Variations 85
Extra Top Variations 85
Color Value Variations 87

11 ❧ Borders 89

12 ❧ Finishing 91
Preparing the Quilt Layers 92
Layering and Basting 93
Quilting 94
Binding 94

Conclusion 95
Suggested Reading 95

About the Authors

NANCY PODOLSKY has always loved to sew just about anything. Around 1987 she became addicted to quilting "because it didn't have to fit a body," and there were so many beautiful fabrics to buy. For 7½ years she owned a quilting and craft store, Oakdale Stitching Post, in Oakdale, California. It was exciting buying and owning thousands of yards of fabric, but there wasn't enough time to pursue her love of sewing, teaching, and being a mom to Sara, David, and Laura. She retired from the retail quilting business in 1993. Traveling, teaching, quilting, and being a mom still keeps Nancy busy. She lives in northern California with husband, Larry, their three children, and four cats.

DEBRA AYERS hated the thought of sewing until the day she taped a quilting show on the television for a friend. She decided that this type of sewing looked "pretty easy." Since that day in 1990, she has made approximately fifty quilts, and likes the challenge of making a design work. While traveling in Oregon, Debra was intrigued by a Bargello Heart design done in fabrics. She took a class during her trip, and when she came home, created, developed, and refined the approach to this fantastic pattern. She shared her creation with Nancy, who asked her to teach a Bargello Heart class at Nancy's shop. Debra successfully taught many classes, inspiring numerous students and even some motorists, who were awestruck by the beautiful quilt samples in the store window. Nancy and Debra decided to collaborate on the development of this book.

SIM AYERS, Debra's husband, is a computer guru and a regular on CompuServe. He originally developed the numerous Layout Plans in this book for Debra to use as teaching aids. Without these charts, creating a Bargello Heart quilt would not be so simple. Prior to this undertaking, Sim knew nothing about designing a quilt. He has since developed a Bargello Heart design program for the computer. Sim and Debra live in northern California and are parents to Erik, Sabrina, and Brian, and proud grandparents of Scotty.

1

Introduction

The same techniques that are used to create Bargello Quilt designs—using simple strips of fabric, sewn together and moved around, to create deep valleys and rounded hills—easily produce the deep valley and rounded hills of a symmetrical heart design. The fabric colors can be selected to radiate out in strong vibrant waves of color from the center, or can be a soft diffused halo created by a gradual blend of numerous shades and prints. The motion of the heart image and the use of color keep the eye interested and constantly moving through the areas of the design to absorb it all.

This book will take you through the process of creating a Bargello Heart step by step: selecting the fabrics, choosing a quilt size, and cutting and sewing the fabrics together. Pressing, counter-cutting, and assembly techniques specific to this design are covered in detail. A simple fabric numbering system and detailed Layout Plans for each quilt size make the construction and design procedures effortless. There is also a chapter with suggestions for finishing and quilting your Bargello Heart.

Warning! Making Bargello Heart Quilts is habit forming. Almost everyone in my classes found they could not stop with just one. They had to design and create "just one more," using different color variations to see yet another effect.

The Bargello Heart process consists of four main tasks: cutting fabric strips, assembling strata units, making counter-cuts, and arranging and sewing the counter-cuts. Review all the instructions in this book before you start; being familiar with the whole process will help you with each step along the way.

Cutting Fabric Strips

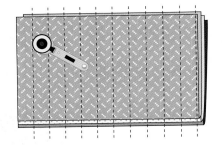

First choose the quilt size you would like to make. Then select, arrange, and number 12 different fabrics. Each fabric will be cut into a specified number of strips. See Chapter 2, "Supplies," for quilt sizes. Chapter 3, "Fabric Selection," covers choosing and arranging your fabrics. Chapter 4, "Cutting Fabric Strips," deals with cutting techniques and lists the specific strip widths you will need.

Assembling Strata Units

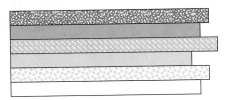

A strata is simply one unit of fabric created by sewing strips of several fabrics together. Chapter 5, "Strata Construction," discusses how to sew and press the fabric strips together into strata units, and lists the number of identical strata units needed for each quilt size.

Making Counter-Cuts

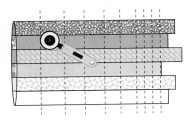

Counter-cuts are units that are cut from the strata, perpendicular to the strata seams. The widths of the counter-cuts and the number of each needed vary depending on the quilt size. See Chapter 6, "Counter-Cuts," for details about cutting techniques and the specific counter-cuts required for your quilt size.

Assembling the Bargello Heart from Counter-Cuts

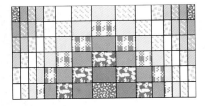

The counter-cuts are laid out and sewn together in sections, according to a specific plan. The sections are sewn together to create the heart design. Chapter 7 discusses the Bargello Heart construction, and includes the Basic Layout Plan and specific assembly instructions for the Basic size. Chapter 8 provides Layout Plans and specific instructions for the Twin, Full, and Queen sizes. Chapter 9 discusses and includes Layout Plans for the Mini, Baby, and King sizes.

More About Layout Plans

Designates counter-cut width

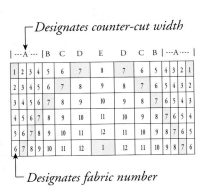

Designates fabric number

As you arrange your 12 fabrics, each is assigned a number from 1 to 12 (this is discussed in Chapter 4). The Fabric Chart on page 18 will help you keep track of these fabrics and their numbers. The Layout Plans in Chapters 7, 8, and 9 use numbered boxes that correspond to the numbers on the fabric chart. Each row of numbered boxes also has a letter above it that corresponds to the width of the counter-cut. As you read the assembly instructions for the quilt size you are creating, follow its Layout Plan carefully.

2

Supplies

EQUIPMENT LIST

To create a Bargello Heart quilt, you will need:

- a rotary cutter, mat, and acrylic ruler. These are helpful tools, and speed up the preparation time considerably. Scissors are a time-consuming substitute.

- a sewing machine that you are familiar with. Be sure it is in good working condition.

- a ¼" patchwork foot for your sewing machine. This type of foot helps you sew accurate seams, and is available for most brands of sewing machines.

- a machine quilting foot (also known as an "even feed" or "walking" foot). This is only necessary if you will be machine quilting your Bargello Heart.

- sewing thread and standard sewing equipment, including a seam ripper, scissors, and pins.

- 400–500 safety pins (size 1) if you will be pin basting the quilt layers. This method is optional; see note on page 93.

CHOOSING A QUILT SIZE

Begin your Bargello Heart project by choosing a quilt size. Many quilters feel that starting with a Baby or a Mini size quilt will be easier since it is smaller in size. However, constructing these sizes requires precision sewing and lots of patience. Because some of the smaller counter-cuts are ¾" and 1" wide, sewing them together can prove difficult. I recommend starting with the Basic size since it involves wider counter-cuts and is therefore easier for a first project.

Quilt Sizes

	Basic	Twin	Full	Queen	Mini	Baby	King
Quilt Size Without Borders	53" x 60"	47" x 76"	53" x 76"	60" x 80"	21" x 29"	36" x 45"	80" x 80"
Quilt Size With Borders	74" x 81"	68" x 97"	74" x 97"	81" x 101"	29" x 37"	43" x 55"	110" x 110"
Standard Mattress Sizes	—	39" x 75"	54" x 75"	60" x 80"	—	27" x 52"	76" x 80"

PURCHASING THE FABRIC

Before purchasing your fabric, read Chapter 3, "Fabric Selection." This chapter discusses general Bargello Heart design concepts and provides tips for choosing and arranging the fabrics and colors in your quilt.

Yardage Requirements

	Basic	Twin	Full	Queen	Mini	Baby	King
Heart Design—12 Fabrics (yardage shown is per fabric)	½ yd. (x12)	½ yd. (x12)	⅝ yd. (x12)	⅔ yd. (x12)	⅙ yd. (x12)	⅓ yd. (x12)	⅔ yd. (x12)
First Border	½ yd.	½ yd.	½ yd.	⅝ yd.	⅙ yd.	—	¾ yd.
Second Border	⅔ yd.	⅔ yd.	⅔ yd.	1 yd.	—	—	1⅜ yd.
Third Border	1⅜ yd.	1⅜ yd.	1⅜ yd.	1⅝ yd.	½ yd.	⅝ yd.	1¾ yd.
Binding	¾ yd.	¾ yd.	¾ yd.	1 yd.	½ yd.	½ yd.	1⅛ yd.
Backing Fabric	5 yd.	5½ yd.	5¾ yd.	6½ yd.	1 yd.	2 yd.	9¾ yd.

Note: All yardage is given for 44" wide fabric.

BATTING

When your quilt top is finished, measure it and buy a packaged batt, or batting off the roll, that is at least 4" longer and 4" wider than the top. My preference is Hobbs Heirloom® cotton batting. I like the ease of quilting with this type of batt. It can be quilted up to 3" apart, has a soft hand, and when washed reminds me of the comfy look of an antique quilt.

MORE ABOUT TOOLS

Using quality tools will make quilt construction quicker and easier. The biggest innovations to the world of quilting since the introduction of the sewing machine are rotary cutters, self-healing mats, and clear acrylic rulers. The speed and accuracy of these cutting tools make scissors almost unnecessary.

There are different brands available for each of the tools mentioned, with varying quality, features, and prices. Ask fellow quilters which brands they prefer and why. If possible, try not to let price be the determining factor for your choice. I have seen too many students choose the least expensive brands, only to later wish they had spent more for a brand with better features.

Rotary Cutters

The rotary cutter resembles a pizza cutter with its round and extremely sharp blade. When the safety cover is retracted and the blade is exposed, it will easily cut through several layers as you press down and roll it across the fabric. Be very respectful of the blade as it is made of surgical steel and cuts fingers as easily as fabric. I personally prefer the following brands:

Olfa® rotary cutters have a protective blade cover that is manually pulled back out of the way. This way, the cover will not push against the layers of fabric and cause them to shift when cutting. Olfa® cutters are available in several sizes.

Fiskars® rotary cutters have an opening in the handle for the fingers to grip. This keeps the fingers together and away from the blade. *If a younger person will be using the rotary cutter, this would be my choice.* This cutter is more comfortable for people with wrist problems, since the handle is at a slight angle to the blade. The blade moves from one side of the cutter to the other, making it easy to use either left-handed or right-handed. The protective cover on this rotary cutter is also manually retractable, therefore it does not push on the fabric layers when cutting.

> ### Hint
>
> *It is wise to permanently identify your equipment with your name. In a classroom all the equipment looks the same. If your tools are labeled, the shop owner will be able to contact you if you should leave one behind. I cannot tell you how many pairs of scissors accumulated at my shop because there were no names and I could not call their owners.*

Cutting Mats

When using rotary cutters it is necessary to use a special cutting mat. Rotary cutting mats are made from a self-healing material that protects the table surface and keeps the rotary cutting blade from becoming dull. The blade penetrates the mat, which "heals" or goes back together once the blade passes, leaving no mark. Cutting mats are available in different sizes. The 18" x 24" size is popular for class use because it is easy to transport. The 24" x 36" size is favored for home use because it is large enough to cut the full width of fabric. I like Olfa® cutting mats because they heal well and are also easy on blades. These mats will not show wear as quickly as other brands.

Rulers

A clear acrylic ruler, approximately ¼" thick, becomes a guide for the rotary cutter. The blade of the cutter is positioned against the edge of the ruler so that it glides along the straight edge. The lines on the ruler make it easy to quickly measure and cut a variety of straight, accurate strip widths. A project that would take hours to mark by hand and cut with scissors takes only minutes to measure and cut with a rotary cutter, acrylic ruler, and mat.

Omnigrid,® I truly feel, makes the best rulers for accuracy, durability, and versatility. These rulers have yellow and black lines, so that the measurements and markings show on either dark or light fabrics. The numbers are easy to read, and the many measuring lines help ensure accuracy. In all the years I have been using my Omnigrid® rulers, I have never had any line markings wear off, and mine have definitely gotten a workout. On the other hand, marking lines did wear off on other brands I used.

MORE ABOUT FABRIC

First, purchase top quality fabrics. The many hours spent making this quilt are well worth the investment. Even with the best construction skills, a quilt cannot become better than the quality of the fabric purchased.

Whether or not to prewash fabrics is widely debated. Some people prefer to prewash fabrics to wash away any applied finishes and extra dye, and to pre-shrink the fabrics. I personally do not feel it necessary to prewash fabrics when making quilts. If I am worried that a color may run, I test a small piece in warm water to see if it is colorfast. If there is color visible in the warm water, I wash the fabric to see if the excess color washes out completely. Then I test the fabric again for colorfastness. If the fabric is not colorfast, I do not use it.

Most 100% cotton fabric will shrink a bit when washed. When using un-washed fabric, I feel steam ironing it will take care of most of the shrinkage.

3

Fabric Selection

Each Bargello Heart design, for any of the quilt sizes, begins with the selection of 12 fabrics. Don't panic at the thought of picking out 12 different fabrics. It is easier than you think, and by the second or third Bargello Heart quilt you won't give it another thought! This chapter covers the many factors to consider when choosing and arranging the fabrics for the Bargello Heart design.

If you have not already done so, decide which quilt size you will be creating. The charts on page 8 provide the dimensions and yardage requirements for the quilt sizes covered in this book. The yardage amounts given are sufficient for each size and also include a small extra allowance. Remember to purchase extra yardage if you vary the pattern in any way. I recommend starting with the Basic size. Since it is on the smaller side (53" x 60"), the project is easy to handle and uses a moderate amount of fabric.

Overview

In general, choose 100% cotton fabrics as they are the easiest to cut, sew, and press. If you are uncertain about color combinations, a good resource is the staff at the local quilt shop. They are familiar with combining numerous fabric colors together for a quilt. By supporting your local quilt shop, you will ensure that it stays in business and will continue to provide new and creative classes with inspirational teachers. (That is how this book came to life!) Such classes encourage and support the creative talents in all of us.

FABRIC COLOR AND DESIGN CHOICES

First, choose a feature fabric that includes two or more colors you like. This fabric is *usually* used for one of the quilt borders as well. Fabrics with large colorful prints, paisleys, floral designs, or just multi-swirls of color are good choices. Then choose two different color families to go with this feature fabric.

The remaining 11 fabrics should go with one of the two color families you selected to emphasize. These do not necessarily need to be mono-colored fabrics, but should primarily feature a color from one of the two families. Pick out fabrics in light, medium, and dark values in each of the color families. There should be a definite change of value between the fabrics, so that the colors do not blend together and look flat.

The "standard" arrangement described in the next section has 6 fabrics in each color family. The feature fabric is incorporated into either of the two color groups. So for this arrangement, you would need 6 fabrics for one color family, and 5 fabrics, plus the feature fabric, for the second color family. (Modifications to this grouping are covered in Chapter 10, "Design Variations.")

Selecting fabrics in a variety of print sizes adds interest to a quilt. Be adventuresome and use a fabric that you ordinarily would not use. I call this a "risky" fabric. A risky fabric is one you customarily would not choose because the design or color(s) are not ones you typically pick out. However, such a fabric can add a sparkle.

Directional fabrics are also fun to use. Directional fabrics have a printed design going in one direction. **Special instructions on page 25 give specific sewing instructions for using directional fabrics.** This information should be followed closely so that the directional fabric does not end up being upside down in the bottom area of the heart shape.

> ## Hint
>
> *Using a red viewing lens will help determine the value differences between several fabrics when they are next to each other.*

ARRANGING THE FABRICS

The heart shape of the design is made prominent by the arrangement of the fabrics. The following sections guide you through grouping the 12 fabrics to achieve a pleasant effect. There are several ways to arrange the fabrics. In each case the fabrics are assembled in a specific order. First the fabrics are divided into color families. Then each color family is sorted by value, for example, dark to light. Different visual effects result from how the color value order is manipulated.

The Standard Arrangement

The "standard" arrangement is the one I teach most often in my classes. (Other arrangements are covered in Chapter 10, Design Variations.) In it, I shade from one color group to the other, from dark to light then light to dark. The feature fabric is incorporated into one of these runs, in the color family where it fits best. To begin, set your fabrics in front of you and arrange the two color families by value from dark to light.

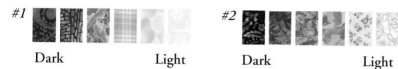

Place one group on the left side, keeping the values in order from dark to light. The other group is placed to the right of this group. Switch the value run, keeping them in order, so that the values shade from light to dark. This is the "standard" value arrangement.

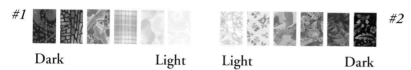

Step back and check to make sure that there is a definite value change between each fabric. If the values blend too closely, the heart shape becomes undefined or mushy. Another point to keep in mind is that the first dark fabric in line, at one end (A), will end up appearing next to the last dark fabric in line, at the other end (B).

A   B

Once all the fabrics are lined up in a pleasing order, decide which fabric you would like to see in the **V** that is formed at the exact center of the Bargello Heart. Usually one of the lighter fabrics is chosen (*), but a dark fabric can also be used.

*

Next, determine which of the fabrics on either side of the **V** fabric, the fabric to the immediate right (a) or left (b), you would like to see "surrounding" the **V**. When the heart is constructed, this fabric will appear to enclose the **V** fabric.

a   *   b

Hint

Refer to Figure 1, on page 15, to see where the "center V" and "surrounding" fabrics will end up in the finished heart design.

Assigning Fabric Numbers

The next step is to assign a number to each fabric (keeping the fabrics in the established order), from #1 through #12. As each fabric is numbered, check to see where it appears in the finished heart design illustrated on the following page. The fabrics in the illustration (Figure 1) are arranged from dark to light/light to dark, as discussed in this section.

The center **V** fabric is assigned #7. The fabric that is chosen to surround it is assigned #6. These two fabrics together form the central area of the heart.

The fabrics on the other side of #6 are assigned numbers in descending order from #5 to #1. They form the inner area of the heart image.

The fabrics on the other side of #7 are assigned #8 through #12, and form the outer area of the heart.

Now, arrange the fabrics so that they are in order, from left to right, #1 through #12. Switch the fabrics to opposite sides, if necessary.

Arrangement Variations

The **V** fabric (#7) does not necessarily need to be one of the fabrics in the center of the value run. If you choose a fabric toward one end, for example, the look of the heart will change, but the numbering procedure is the same. First choose the #7 and #6 fabrics, then number the rest accordingly.

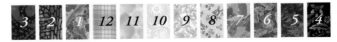

Finally, switch the fabrics around so that they are in sequence from left to right.

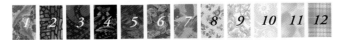

See Chapter 10, "Design Variations," for illustrations of some different fabric value arrangements.

Figure 1 How fabric numbers correspond to the areas of the heart image

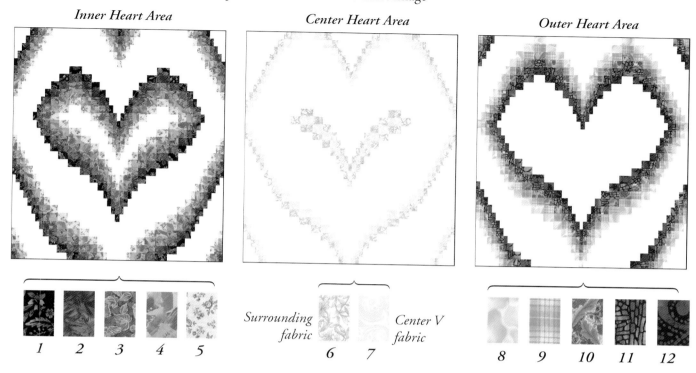

Inner Heart Area | Center Heart Area | Outer Heart Area

1 2 3 4 5

Surrounding fabric   Center V fabric

6 7

8 9 10 11 12

The Inner, Center, and Outer areas, shown above with their numbered fabric swatches, form this complete Bargello Heart image when put together.

It is safe to say that if you have chosen 12 fabrics you like and that look good together, your Bargello Heart Quilt will be striking no matter how you arrange the fabrics. However, some arrangements will please you more than others. Here are some ideas and tools to help you visualize the finished heart before you start to cut and sew.

The Bargello Heart Gallery

Now that the process of choosing and arranging the fabrics has been explained, a "real-life" case may further help you visualize how the fabrics will look in a heart design. For a full color illustration and explanation of a fabric arrangement and the resulting quilt design, see "A Sample Color Arrangement" on page 32. This section describes the process of choosing and numbering the fabrics for the first quilt in the "Bargello Heart Gallery."

Many of the quilts in the "Bargello Heart Gallery" are based on the standard fabric arrangement that is described on the previous pages. Others use arrangements that are quite different. Study the quilts in this section to see how color groupings and shading variations affect the look of a quilt.

Areas of the Heart Image

The illustration on page 15 shows three distinct areas of the Bargello Heart image along with the fabric numbers that correspond to them. As you "try out" different arrangements, refer to this page and imagine where each of your fabrics will appear in the quilt. Fabric placement defines the color sequencing in the heart.

The Blank Layout Plan

Use the blank Layout Plan on the facing page as a further aid in planning your Bargello Heart. Try out different color and value placements by filling in the numbered boxes with colored pencils. No matter what size quilt you are creating, you can use this chart to help you visualize the finished design. Your project may use more or fewer rows, but the color movement will remain the same. Use the "key" below the chart to assign and keep track of the colors.

Value Arrangements

As mentioned before, the fabric value arrangement plays a big role in the look of a Bargello Heart Quilt. Chapter 10, "Design Variations," offers three more ways to arrange the values, and shows how the changes affect the appearance of the heart design.

Hint

Photocopy the Blank Layout Plan so that you can use it with future Bargello Heart projects.

BLANK LAYOUT PLAN

9	10	11	12	1	2	3	4	5	6	7	8	7	6	5	4	3	2	1	2	3	4	5	6	7	8	7	6	5	4	3	2	1	12	11	10	9
10	11	12	1	2	3	4	5	6	7	8	9	8	7	6	5	4	3	2	3	4	5	6	7	8	9	8	7	6	5	4	3	2	1	12	11	10
11	12	1	2	3	4	5	6	7	8	9	10	9	8	7	6	5	4	3	4	5	6	7	8	9	10	9	8	7	6	5	4	3	2	1	12	11
12	1	2	3	4	5	6	7	8	9	10	11	10	9	8	7	6	5	4	5	6	7	8	9	10	11	10	9	8	7	6	5	4	3	2	1	12
1	2	3	4	5	6	7	8	9	10	11	12	11	10	9	8	7	6	5	6	7	8	9	10	11	12	11	10	9	8	7	6	5	4	3	2	1
2	3	4	5	6	7	8	9	10	11	12	1	12	11	10	9	8	7	6	7	8	9	10	11	12	1	12	11	10	9	8	7	6	5	4	3	2
3	4	5	6	7	8	9	10	11	12	1	2	1	12	11	10	9	8	7	8	9	10	11	12	1	2	1	12	11	10	9	8	7	6	5	4	3
4	5	6	7	8	9	10	11	12	1	2	3	2	1	12	11	10	9	8	9	10	11	12	1	2	3	2	1	12	11	10	9	8	7	6	5	4
5	6	7	8	9	10	11	12	1	2	3	4	3	2	1	12	11	10	9	10	11	12	1	2	3	4	3	2	1	12	11	10	9	8	7	6	5
6	7	8	9	10	11	12	1	2	3	4	5	4	3	2	1	12	11	10	11	12	1	2	3	4	5	4	3	2	1	12	11	10	9	8	7	6
7	8	9	10	11	12	1	2	3	4	5	6	5	4	3	2	1	12	11	12	1	2	3	4	5	6	5	4	3	2	1	12	11	10	9	8	7
8	9	10	11	12	1	2	3	4	5	6	7	6	5	4	3	2	1	12	1	2	3	4	5	6	7	6	5	4	3	2	1	12	11	10	9	8
7	8	9	10	11	12	1	2	3	4	5	6	7	6	5	4	3	2	1	2	3	4	5	6	7	6	5	4	3	2	1	12	11	10	9	8	7
6	7	8	9	10	11	12	1	2	3	4	5	6	7	6	5	4	3	2	3	4	5	6	7	6	5	4	3	2	1	12	11	10	9	8	7	6
5	6	7	8	9	10	11	12	1	2	3	4	5	6	7	6	5	4	3	4	5	6	7	6	5	4	3	2	1	12	11	10	9	8	7	6	5
4	5	6	7	8	9	10	11	12	1	2	3	4	5	6	7	6	5	4	5	6	7	6	5	4	3	2	1	12	11	10	9	8	7	6	5	4
3	4	5	6	7	8	9	10	11	12	1	2	3	4	5	6	7	6	5	6	7	6	5	4	3	2	1	12	11	10	9	8	7	6	5	4	3
2	3	4	5	6	7	8	9	10	11	12	1	2	3	4	5	6	7	6	7	6	5	4	3	2	1	12	11	10	9	8	7	6	5	4	3	2
1	2	3	4	5	6	7	8	9	10	11	12	1	2	3	4	5	6	7	6	5	4	3	2	1	12	11	10	9	8	7	6	5	4	3	2	1
12	1	2	3	4	5	6	7	8	9	10	11	12	1	2	3	4	5	6	5	4	3	2	1	12	11	10	9	8	7	6	5	4	3	2	1	12
11	12	1	2	3	4	5	6	7	8	9	10	11	12	1	2	3	4	5	4	3	2	1	12	11	10	9	8	7	6	5	4	3	2	1	12	11
10	11	12	1	2	3	4	5	6	7	8	9	10	11	12	1	2	3	4	3	2	1	12	11	10	9	8	7	6	5	4	3	2	1	12	11	10
9	10	11	12	1	2	3	4	5	6	7	8	9	10	11	12	1	2	1	2	1	12	11	10	9	8	7	6	5	4	3	2	1	12	11	10	9
8	9	10	11	12	1	2	3	4	5	6	7	8	9	10	11	12	1	2	1	12	11	10	9	8	7	6	5	4	3	2	1	12	11	10	9	8
7	8	9	10	11	12	1	2	3	4	5	6	7	8	9	10	11	12	1	12	11	10	9	8	7	6	5	4	3	2	1	12	11	10	9	8	7
6	7	8	9	10	11	12	1	2	3	4	5	6	7	8	9	10	11	12	11	10	9	8	7	6	5	4	3	2	1	12	11	10	9	8	7	6
5	6	7	8	9	10	11	12	1	2	3	4	5	6	7	8	9	10	11	10	9	8	7	6	5	4	3	2	1	12	11	10	9	8	7	6	5
4	5	6	7	8	9	10	11	12	1	2	3	4	5	6	7	8	9	10	9	8	7	6	5	4	3	2	1	12	11	10	9	8	7	6	5	4
3	4	5	6	7	8	9	10	11	12	1	2	3	4	5	6	7	8	9	8	7	6	5	4	3	2	1	12	11	10	9	8	7	6	5	4	3
2	3	4	5	6	7	8	9	10	11	12	1	2	3	4	5	6	7	8	7	6	5	4	3	2	1	12	11	10	9	8	7	6	5	4	3	2

Use colored pencils to approximate your fabric choices in the numbered key at right. Then color in the heart design above to help you see how the colors and values will radiate throughout the heart design.

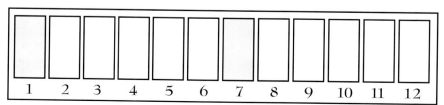

1 2 3 4 5 6 7 8 9 10 11 12

Hint

Photocopy the Fabric Charts so that you can use them with future Bargello Heart projects.

After you have arranged and numbered your fabrics, cut a small swatch of each and tape it in the appropriately numbered box on one of the Fabric Charts below. A fabric chart makes it easy to remember the number assigned to each fabric. You will refer to this chart many times during the creation of your quilt.

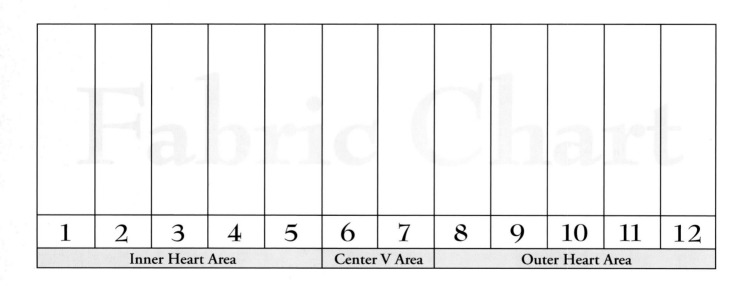

1	2	3	4	5	6	7	8	9	10	11	12
Inner Heart Area					Center V Area		Outer Heart Area				

1	2	3	4	5	6	7	8	9	10	11	12
Inner Heart Area					Center V Area		Outer Heart Area				

Cutting Fabric Strips

Once the fabric is chosen, it is time to iron and cut it into strips. The Bargello Heart is created exclusively with equal-width strips cut from 12 different fabrics. A rotary cutter, an acrylic ruler, and a mat are best suited for cutting the strips quickly and accurately. Detailed information about these products is located in Chapter 2, "Supplies."

FABRIC PREPARATION

Ironing

Before cutting, iron the fabrics to remove any wrinkles. Ironing with a steam iron also pre-shrinks unwashed fabric. Using spray starch while ironing will restore the "body" to prewashed fabrics. If the fabric has good body, it is easier to handle as you cut and sew the strips together, and also later when the seams are pressed.

Folding

The strips of fabric are cut perpendicular to the folded edge of the fabric. The folded edge is parallel to the selvage or woven edges. If the original fold is not straight, open up the fabric and iron out the old fold. Then refold the fabric in half, and press a new straight fold. (Under no condition should strips of fabric be torn for this project.) Fold the fabric in half, with the selvage edges together, keeping the fold nearest to you. Make sure the fabric lies smooth on the cutting mat, with no wrinkles or twists. The excess fabric should lie to the right if you are right-handed, or to the left if you are left-handed.

Layering

If the fabrics are folded only once, several fabrics can be layered on top of each other. This way more than one fabric can be cut at a time. (I recommend this technique only after you are comfortable using rotary cutting equipment.) Fold each fabric once, then stack the fabrics one on top of the other, so that the folds are parallel and about ¼" of each fabric shows. Do not let the stack of fabrics exceed the ruler length (24" maximum). The cutting will not be accurate if you have to move the ruler up or down in order to cut the full length of the strips.

Rotary cutters can easily cut through eight layers of fabric (four fabrics folded once each). Use a rotary cutter with a manually retractable blade guard, such as the Olfa® brand. Self-retractable rotary cutters, such as the Dritz® brand, rely on the fabric to push the guard back. If you attempt to cut a stack of fabrics with this type of rotary cutter, it will move the top layers of fabric. Take care that all folded edges remain parallel while cutting. Check the folds often with your ruler and realign when necessary.

Figure 2 Fabrics folded once and layered on top of each other

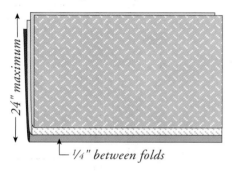

24" maximum

¼" between folds

Fabric can be folded once and cut as described, or it can be folded a second time to shorten the cutting distance. Many people find it easier to hold the ruler steady for a shorter cutting distance. After folding the fabric the first time, carefully fold it a second time by bringing the first fold up and matching it to the selvage edges. Take care during the folding process to keep all the folds parallel and the fabric smooth and flat. If the folds are not parallel, the strips will have a V at each fold.

Figure 3 Fabric folded a second time

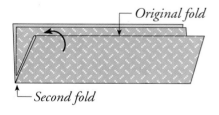

Original fold

Second fold

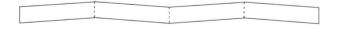

CUTTING TECHNIQUE

The first cut is a "clean-up" cut. This cut is made to create a straight edge perpendicular to the fold. The remaining cuts, the actual fabric strips, are cut parallel to this edge, so that they are straight and uniform.

The Clean-Up Cut

The easiest way to make a clean-up cut is by using two rulers. Place one ruler on top of the fabric near the edge where the first cut will be made. Position one of the short lines of the ruler along the folded edge of the fabric. With the hand you hold the cutter in, firmly hold the ruler in place (Figure 4A). Position the longer ruler against the long edge of the first ruler and hold the second ruler firmly in place (Figure 4B). Remove the first ruler and run the rotary cutter along the edge of the second ruler to make the first cut, the clean-up cut (Figure 4C).

To achieve straight cuts, it is important that the ruler be held firmly in place. If the ruler moves while the fabric is being cut, either the edges will not be parallel, or the strips will be different widths in different places. Spread your fingers and thumb apart on top of the ruler surface. Fingers over the edge of the ruler can get sliced! Note the hand positions in Figure 5, on the following page.

Use your finger pads to press down and hold the ruler firmly in place while cutting. By using the pads of the fingers, instead of the flat area of the hand, it is easy to move your hand along the ruler in a "walking" motion. I cut the same distance that my hand is covering on the ruler, stop cutting, then "walk" my hand carefully up the ruler to the next area to be cut.

Figure 4 Making a clean-up cut

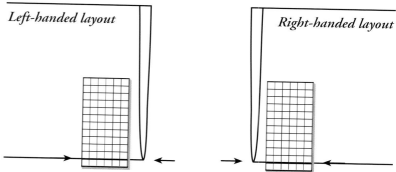

A) *Position small ruler just inside fabric edge and align a horizontal grid line on the fold.*

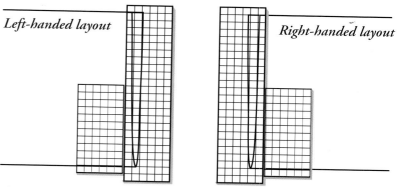

B) *Hold the small ruler firmly in place while butting the large ruler along its edge.*

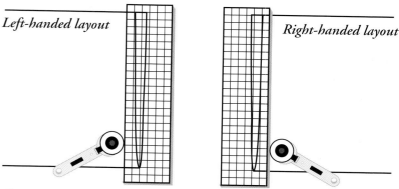

C) *Remove the small ruler and make the clean-up cut along the inside edge of the large ruler.*

Keeping your hand on the ruler, in the same area that is being cut, keeps the ruler from sliding around. Never cut against the edge of the ruler unless your hand is in position, with pressure holding the ruler down firmly on the fabric.

Note: It is essential that the clean-up cut is perpendicular to the fold. If it is not, the cut strips of fabric will have a V at the fold when the strip is opened:

If the strips are not cut straight, it becomes difficult to sew them together accurately. A beginner using the rotary cutter should make a clean-up cut after every third strip has been cut. Always check the cut edge to see that it remains straight and *perpendicular to the folded edge.* If the ruler slips while cutting a strip, stop and make a clean-up cut. (See Figure 4.)

Cutting Strips

To cut the desired strip width, place the long edge of the ruler over the cut edge of the fabric. Because the acrylic ruler is clear, you can see through it to line up the markings with the edge of the fabric. Move the ruler over the fabric to the desired strip width. Check that a short line of the ruler is along the fold, and a long line is along the cut edge. This will ensure that a perfectly straight strip of fabric is cut. Continue moving the ruler across the fabric and cutting the necessary number of strips. (The cutting mat always needs to be under the blade so that the table surface does not get cut.) Recheck the cut edge of the fabric periodically to make sure it is still perpendicular to the fold. Realign with a clean-up cut when necessary.

The chart below shows the strip width and the number of strips to cut from each of the twelve fabrics for each quilt size covered in this book.

Figure 5 Cutting a strip

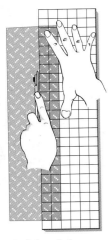

Left-handed cut

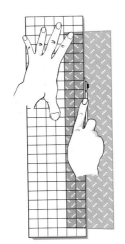

Right-handed cut

Strip Cutting Chart

	Basic	Twin	Full	Queen	Mini	Baby	King
Strip Width	2½"	2½"	2½"	2½"	1½"	2"	3"
Number of Strips to Cut (from each of 12 fabrics)	5	6	7	8	3	4	7

5

Strata Construction

Rather than sewing small individual pieces of fabric together, as is done in traditional quilt making, the Bargello style uses strata units made by sewing strips of fabric together. These strata units are then ironed and cut, or "counter-cut," perpendicular to the seams. This way, you never need to handle or organize tiny pieces of fabric. The term "strata" was first introduced to me in a class taught by Marilyn Doheny. A strata is simply strips of fabric sewn together along their long edges to make a single unit.

Figure 6 A strata unit

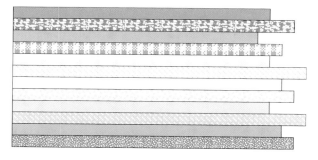

Due to manufacturing processes, fabrics vary greatly in width: the fabric on a "45-inch" bolt can actually be anywhere from 42" (occasionally narrower) to 46." Therefore, always start sewing the strips from the same end. This way one end of the strata ends up fairly even. If any of the fabrics are narrower than 42",

you may not get the necessary number of counter-cuts. This is easily solved by making one more strata unit. There should be enough leftover fabric to make at least one additional strata.

The strata units for all quilt sizes are made from 12 different fabrics. After reviewing the strata construction procedures that follow, you will sew the fabric strips together to create the number of identical strata units needed for your quilt size. The chart below shows the number of identical strata units needed to complete the quilt sizes discussed in this book.

Strata Unit Chart

	Basic	Twin	Full	Queen	Mini	Baby	King
Number of Identical Stata Units to Create for Each Quilt Size	5	6	7	8	3	4	7

Note: If you find that any of your fabrics are narrower than 42", make one more strata than listed above.

SEWING AND PRESSING

Sewing Consistent Seam Allowances

When sewing the strips together, a consistent seam allowance is imperative so that the seam junctions of the pattern will fit together as they are sewn. The Bargello Heart design is sewn together with a ¼" seam allowance. A ¼" seam may be obtained by using the edge of the presser foot as a guide. If your machine sews a little wider or a little narrower ¼" seam, that will be okay, just be consistent and use the same machine and settings for the whole project. A ¼" patchwork foot is available for most sewing machines from a sewing machine dealer. There are also generic presser feet available at some quilt shops.

If you cannot get an exact ¼" seam, your quilt top will be smaller or larger than stated in this book, but the seams will match if all of the seam allowances are at least identical throughout the piecing of the strata units.

Pressing the Seams

The next step is to start sewing the strips together. Let's go over the pressing process first, though, as sewing and pressing happen in conjunction with one another. After each seam is sewn it is then pressed. This step is as important as cutting the strips straight and sewing with a consistent seam allowance.

Iron across the seam or strata unit on the front side. This allows the edge of the iron to work open any little pleats that might appear at the seam line. The seam allowances are pressed so that both sides lie together on the same side of the seam line. The pressing is done gently with the straight edge of the iron doing the work. *Do not pull or stretch the strata when pressing.* Careful pressing ensures that the quilt parts go together easily and precisely.

USING DIRECTIONAL FABRICS

If you decide to use a directional fabric, you will need to arrange the strips of this fabric differently in order to keep the design moving in the same direction throughout the quilt top. Follow these steps for directional fabrics:

1) In all but two of the strata units, sew the directional fabric with the image in an upward position.

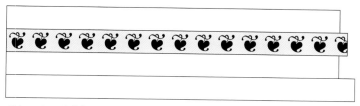

Directional fabric image appears upward in all but two strata units.

2) In two of the strata units, sew the directional fabric upside down.

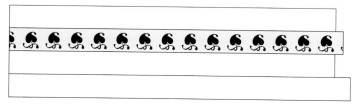

Directional fabric image appears upside down in two strata units.

Label these two "upside down" strata units so they will be easy to identify when you are making the counter-cuts.

3) Use the "upside down" strata units (as shown in Step 2) for making the counter-cuts for the Bottom Section of the heart.

4) In the Center Section of the heart design, the directional fabrics will run in both directions. For this section some of the counter-cuts will also be cut from the "upside down" strata units.

Note: Making counter-cuts is covered in greater depth in Chapter 6, "Counter-Cuts." Arranging the counter-cuts in sections is covered in Chapter 7, "Basic Heart Construction."

Hint

If you run short of counter-cuts that have the correct design orientation, simply remove the directional piece, turn it to the desired direction and resew the piece back into the counter-cut strip.

Refer to the numbers on your fabric chart and sew the strips together as shown below. See "Sewing and Pressing" on page 24 for more about strata construction.

Begin by sewing the strips, right sides together, in pairs: strip #1 to strip #2, strip #3 to strip #4, and so on, as indicated by the plus signs between the strips. Remember to maintain consistent ¼" seam allowances.

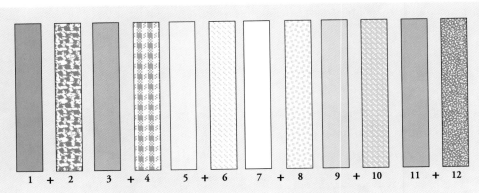

As strips are sewn, press the seams toward the even-numbered fabrics, as indicated by the arrows above each pair.

Now sew the pairs together (#1/#2 to #3/#4, and so on) as indicated by the plus signs between the pairs.

As pairs are sewn into groups of four, press the new seams toward the even-numbered fabrics, as indicated by the arrows above each group.

Now sew the groups together, as indicated by the plus signs between the groups.

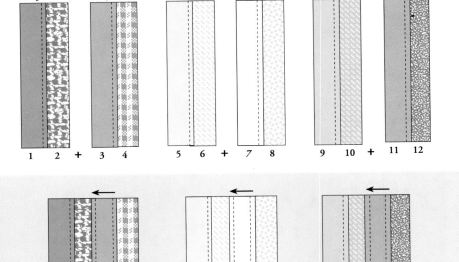

When the groups have been sewn together to complete the strata unit, press the new seams toward the even-numbered fabrics, as indicated by the arrows above the unit. (Only the even-numbered fabrics will have seam allowances under them.)

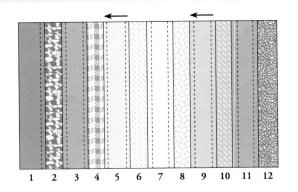

6

Counter-Cuts

The completed strata units are now ready to be cut into counter-cuts, or units that are cut perpendicular to the seams of the strata unit. First, however, the edges of the strata need to be squared to 90° with a clean-up cut. The top and bottom of the strata are then sewn together, resulting in a strata tube. Finally, this tube is cut into the different counter-cut widths needed for your quilt size.

Figure 7 Fold strata in half and make a clean-up cut on one end

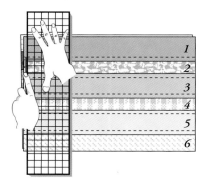

Figure 8 A strata tube

Strata Clean-up Cut

Fold the strata unit in half, along the seam line between fabrics #6 and #7, with the right sides together. Place fabric #1 on top of fabric #12. Make a "clean-up" cut at one end of the strata.

The easiest way to do a clean-up cut is by using two rulers. Place one ruler on top of the fabric near the edge where the first cut will be made. Match one of the short lines of the ruler along the folded edge of the fabric. With the hand you hold the cutter in, firmly hold the ruler in place. Position the other ruler against the long edge of the first ruler and hold the second ruler firmly in place. Remove the first ruler and run the rotary cutter along the edge of the second ruler to make the clean-up cut. (See Figure 4 on page 21.)

Making the Tube

Align fabric strips #1 and #12 at the trimmed end and sew a seam along the long edge. This forms a fabric tube approximately 44" long. Repeat this procedure for each of the strata units needed for the heart size you are making.

CUTTING TECHNIQUE

From the strata tubes, five different widths of counter-cuts will be made. Always counter-cut the *largest* width first, so that any leftovers can be cut at the smaller sizes, thereby utilizing the strata in the most efficient manner. The charts on the opposite page show how many counter-cuts of each width are needed for each quilt size.

As you make your counter-cuts, it is helpful to keep the strips sorted by width in the five different groups. If you have used any directional fabrics, remember to keep counter-cuts made from the "upside-down" strata separate from the rest. See page 25 for details about directional fabrics.

Figure 9 Counter-cut the strata tube, beginning with the largest width

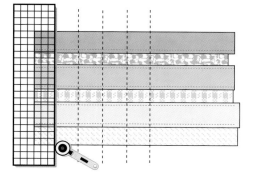

COUNTER-CUT CHARTS

Version 1 Counter-Cuts (Basic, Twin, Full and Queen Sizes)

Counter-Cut Width	3½"	3"	2½"	2"	1½"
Number Needed for Basic Size	6	12	12	12	61
Number needed for Twin Size	8	16	16	16	61
Number needed for Full Size	8	16	16	16	83
Number needed for Queen Size	8	16	16	16	108

Version 2 Counter-Cuts (Mini, Baby and King Sizes)

Counter-Cut Width	4	3½"	3"	2½"	2"	1½"	1"	¾"
Number needed for Mini Size	—	—	—	6	12	12	12	61
Number needed for Baby Size	—	—	6	12	12	12	61	—
Number needed for King Size	6	12	12	12	75	—	—	—

Designated Letters for Counter-Cut Widths

Counter-Cut Letter	A	B	C	D	E
Widths used for Basic, Twin, Full, and Queen Sizes	1½"	2"	2½"	3"	3½"
Widths used for Mini Size	¾"	1"	1½"	2"	2½"
Widths used for Baby Size	1"	1½"	2"	2½"	3"
Widths used for King Size	2"	2½"	3"	3½"	4"

HEART ASSEMBLY PREVIEW

Once the strata tubes are cut into counter-cuts, they will be laid out and assembled to form the heart design. Here is a brief preview of this process:

1. Each counter-cut tube is separated at one of its seams to form a row (Figure 10A). The seam that is separated depends on which fabric is needed at the top of the row.

2. The counter-cut strips are laid out in the order shown on the Layout Plan (Figure 10B).

3. The counter-cuts are sewn together into sections (Figure 10C).

Chapter 7, which follows the "Bargello Heart Gallery," gives complete details about this process, including layout instructions for the Basic size. Chapter 8 covers the Twin, Full, and Queen sizes. Chapter 9 covers the Mini, Baby, and King sizes.

Figure 10 Counter-cut assembly

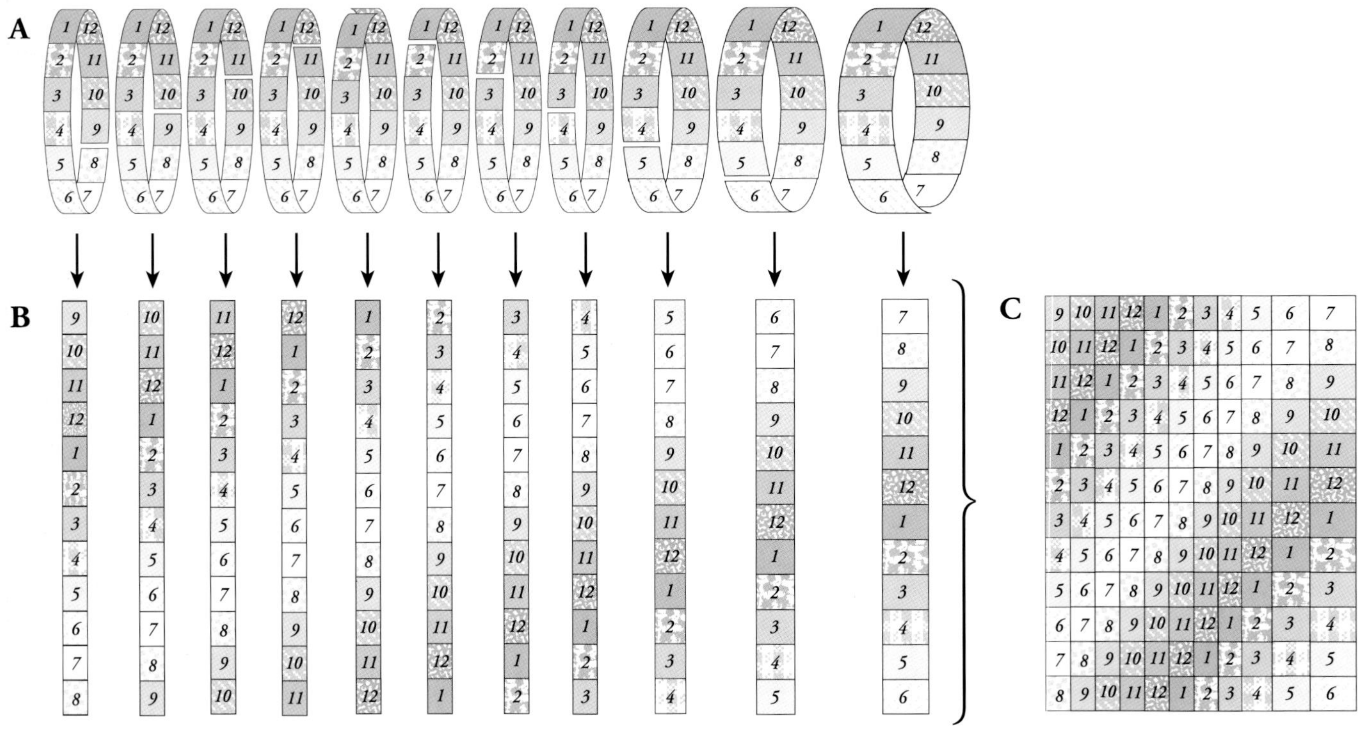

Bargello Heart Gallery

This section contains many stunning examples of Bargello Heart quilts in full color. The variety of design and color combinations will inspire you, and guide the choices you make as you create your very own Bargello Heart quilt.

In addition, the following two pages contain a specific example of how I chose, arranged, and numbered the fabrics for my quilt, *Victorian Dreams.*

When designing *Victorian Dreams,* shown on the opposite page, I began by choosing a feature fabric—a pink floral print on a black background. Pink and black are the two colors I wanted to emphasize and use in the quilt. I chose 11 more fabrics from those two color families to give me a total of 12 fabrics. (See Figure A at right.)

I arranged the fabrics of each color family by value, shading the pink group from dark to light (burgundy to the light pink print), and the black group from light to dark (pale gray print to the dark black prints). The feature fabric was incorporated into the black color family. (See Figure B at right.)

In the quilt, the furthest fabric to the right (Figure B) will appear next to the burgundy fabric at the left end of the sequence. Therefore, I chose a print that included a rose color so that it would blend well with the burgundy.

I decided I wanted the multi-colored pink, blue, and white print to be the V fabric, so I assigned it #7. I wanted the center and inner heart to be pink, so I chose the pink and white check for the surrounding fabric and assigned it #6. The remaining pink fabrics were then numbered in descending order from #5 to #2.

The six fabrics to the right of the V fabric (the black color family) were numbered in ascending order, light to dark, from #8 to #12. The last black print then became the #1 fabric (Figure B). Since I purposely chose a fabric that blends smoothly into the pink group, the flow of colors was continuous. This fabric was moved to the first slot on the left as #1 (Figure C).

With the pink color family on the left of the V fabric, and the black color family on the right, the heart has a pink center shading to a black rim and then shades outward to light gray. If the fabrics were arranged in the opposite order, with the blacks to the left and pinks to the right (Figure D, below) the inner heart would shade from gray to black with a dark burgundy rim, and the outer heart would shade from a dark to a light pink.

D

This fabric arrangement results in a Bargello Heart that shades from gray to black in the middle, instead of pink to burgundy as shown opposite.

The pink color family ranges from a dark burgundy fabric to a tiny pink, blue, and white print. The black color family ranges from a pale gray and white geometric print to black fabrics with floral prints.

The V fabric (#7) and its surrounding fabric (#6) determine the order in which the rest of the fabrics will be numbered.

The last fabric in the black color family was chosen to blend with the burgundy at the other end of the row. This can be thought of as a "transitional" fabric.

Fabric #1 is moved from the end of the row to the beginning, so that the fabrics are in order from #1 to #12. Swatches can now be cut from the fabrics and secured to a Fabric Chart for reference.

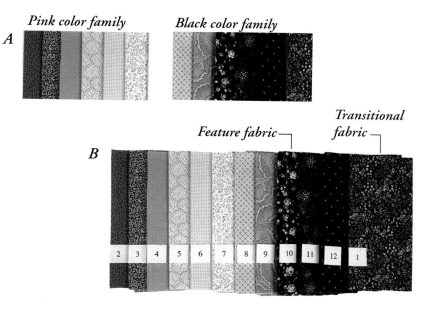

Pink color family　　**Black color family**

A

B　Feature fabric　Transitional fabric

C

1. *Victorian Dreams* by Nancy Podolsky, 64" x 66" (Basic size). Quilted by Norene Michener.

2. *Heart's Desire* by Norene Michener,
63" x 92" (Twin size). In the collection of
Betty Dugand.

3. *Soft and Sweet Memories* by Norene Michener, 42" x 51"
(Baby size). In the collection of Doheny Publications.

*"This Baby size uses the same fabrics as the Twin size above,
but they were used in a slightly different order."*

4. *English Country Garden* by Linda Baird, 67" x 72" (Basic size). Quilted by Darlene Brazil.

5. *Pastel Parfait* by Nancy Podolsky, 41" x 50" (Baby size).

6. *Forever Yours* by Patricia Pulley,
61" x 69" (Basic size).

7. *Stolen Heart* by Nancy Larson, 61" x 66"
(Basic size). In the collection of Emilee
Larson.

*"My daughter Emilee stole my heart the day
she was born, and again she stole my Bargello
Heart Quilt when I made it."*

8. *Brina's Heart* by Debra Ayers, 75" x 97" (Full size). In the collection of Sabrina Ayers.

"My daughter has a love of purples and also loves hearts. There didn't seem to be a question of the design she would choose for her bed. Sabrina also helped choose the fabric."

10. *Country Heart* by Panee Ponder,
67" x 71" (Basic size).

*"I have sewn clothing before, but this was
my first quilt. I had never even used a
rotary cutter!"*

11. *A Heart for Cori* by Diana Fairbanks, 61" x 66" (Basic size). In the collection of Cori Fairbanks.

"This is my second quilt, made with love for my daughter. It has been in her room ever since—she uses it to wrap up in on Saturday mornings to watch cartoons."

12. *15th Anniversary Quilt* by Susan Godkin, 96" x 100" (King size).

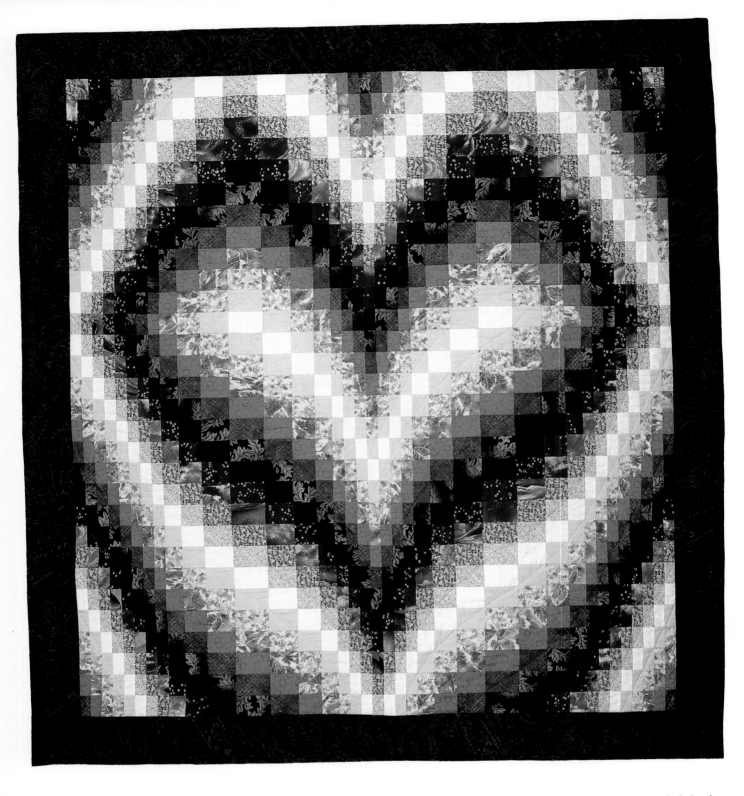

13. *Agua Fresca* by Laura Podolsky (age 13), 62" x 66" (Basic size). In the collection of Sara Podolsky.

"I picked all the colors myself and arranged them. Mom only helped me with the cutting. My sister liked the colors so much that she offered me money—so I took it. This is the second Bargello Heart Quilt I've made. I made my first one when I was 12. I enjoy making the tops, but I don't like doing the quilting!"

14. *Where'd You Get That Dress?*
by Launa Peters, 63" x 70" (Basic size).

"After taking a Bargello workshop with Marilyn Doheny in Oakdale, California, I wanted to try another approach with Bargello. The teals and burgundy colors are a big change from my usual red and black designs. The border fabric was my inspiration for the colors."

15. *Spring Renascence (Rebirth)* by Debra Ayers, 52" x 42" (Baby size).

16. *K.H.K + T.D.K.* by Kathie Koepsell, 74" x 81" (Basic size). Quilted by Patsi Hanseth. In the collection of Doheny Publications.

17. *Dawn Rising* by Susan List, 65" x 71" (Basic size).

"I saw a class sample of a Bargello Heart and decided I would like to make one. I wanted to hang it in my living room, so the fabrics pick up colors in a painting of irises that hangs there. These are my favorite colors. They remind me of the sky as dawn breaks."

 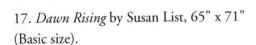

18. *Wild and Crazy Love* by Linda Baird, 67" x 71" (Basic size). Quilted by Darlene Brazil. In the collection of Doheny Publications.

19. *The Wild One* by Nancy Podolsky, 68" x 87" (Twin size).

"I wanted to see what real wild fabric—stripes, dots, etc.—would do in this quilt. To create this Twin size, rows were added to the top and bottom, instead of just the top."

20. *Romance* by Esther Tow-Der, M.D. 68" x 72" (Basic size).

21. *Summer Sunrise* by Debra Ayers, 44" x 54" (Baby size).

22. *Heart in Rhapsody* by Joyce Hamilton, 63" x 70" (Basic size).
In the collection of Doheny Publications.

23. *It's That Time!* by Debra Ayers, 63" x 71" (Basic size).

"Had to see if it could be done using Christmas colors. What fun!"

24. *Transitional Heart* by Joyce Hamilton, 85" x 88" (Queen size).
Quilted by Darlene Brazil. In the collection of Doheny Publications.

25. *Filagree Mosaic* by Norene Michener, 84" x 98" (Queen size). In the collection of Doheny Publications.

"This is a variation of the Queen size with rows added at the bottom and the top. To make the diamonds appear, the Extra Top Variation was used. In addition, the four rows on each end of the Bottom sections were opened in reverse order for diamonds to appear there as well."

7

Basic
Heart Construction

This chapter describes the layout and construction methods that will be used to assemble the counter-cuts into the Bargello Heart design. While this chapter discusses only the Basic size quilt, the same construction methods are used for all Bargello Heart Quilts. Therefore, no matter what size quilt you are creating, read this chapter thoroughly before laying out your counter-cuts or sewing them together.

Specific assembly instructions and Layout Plans for other sizes are located in the next two chapters. Version 1 Quilts (Twin, Full, and Queen sizes) are discussed in Chapter 8. Assembly instructions and Layout Plans for Version 2 Quilts (Mini, Baby, and King sizes) are located in Chapter 9.

Figure 11 Bargello Heart sections

Extra Top (required for some sizes)

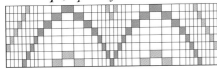

Top

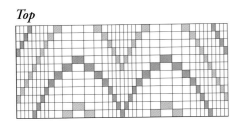

Center

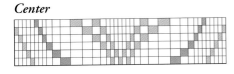

Bottom

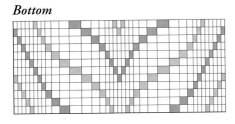

The Bargello Heart quilt top is constructed in three main sections: Top, Center, and Bottom. Some of the quilt sizes require an Extra Top to provide additional length for use on a bed.

Since the Top and the Bottom Sections are constructed in a similar manner, they are made first and second. The Center Section is constructed in a slightly different manner and made after the Top and Bottom Sections. The Extra Top Section is dealt with separately for each quilt size.

Note: Borders are added later so that the finished sizes are big enough to fit standard bed sizes. See Chapter 11, "Borders," for details.

About the Layout Plans

As you read through the instructions for each section, refer to the layout plan that corresponds to the quilt size you have chosen. Across the top of each layout plan are the letters **A**, **B**, **C**, **D**, and **E**, which correspond to the counter-cut width to be used for each row. Below these are row numbers to help you keep the counter-cuts in order as you lay out each section. The number in each box refers to the fabric number. (See Figure 12, below.) Have your fabric chart out for easy reference.

Figure 12 Example of a layout plan

	A		B	C	D	E	D	C	B		A		← Counter-cut width
5	6	7	8	9	10	11	12	13	14	15	16	17 18 19	← Row number
1	2	3	4	5	6	7	8	7	6	5	4	3 2 1	
2	3	4	5	6	7	8	9	8	7	6	5	4 3 2	← Fabric number
3	4	5	6	7	8	9	10	9	8	7	6	5 4 3	
4	5	6	7	8	9	10	11	10	9	8	7	6 5 4	
5	6	7	8	9	10	11	12	11	10	9	8	7 6 5	
6	7	8	9	10	11	12	1	12	11	10	9	8 7 6	
7	8	9	10	11	12	1	2	1	12	11	10	9 8 7	← Shaded boxes help illustrate design movement
8	9	10	11	12	1	2	3	2	1	12	11	10 9 8	
9	10	11	12	1	2	3	4	3	2	1	12	11 10 9	
10	11	12	1	2	3	4	5	4	3	2	1	12 11 10	
11	12	1	2	3	4	5	6	5	4	3	2	1 12 11	
12	1	2	3	4	5	6	7	6	5	4	3	2 1 12	

CONSTRUCTION TECHNIQUE

Laying Out Counter-Cuts

Beginning with row 1 at the left side of each section, choose a counter-cut that matches the width indicated by the letter above that row. Now note the fabric number in the first box of that row. Remove a seam from your counter-cut tube so that the counter-cut starts with the appropriate fabric, and all fabric numbers in the row match those on the layout plan.

Note: These are general instructions for laying out the Bargello Heart design. Specific details for each section of each quilt size can be found later in this chapter, and in Chapters 8 and 9.

Sewing and Pressing

When you have a number of rows laid out, begin sewing them together in pairs as you did when making the strata units. That is, sew row 1 to 2, row 3 to 4, and so forth. Continue laying out the rows and sewing them together in pairs. Then sew the pairs together into groups of four. Sew these units together until each section is complete.

When sewing the rows together, notice how the pieces "lock" together at the seam junctions with the seams of the next row (Figure 13). Remember that as the strata strips were sewn together, the seams were pressed toward the even numbered fabric. Pressing the strata in this manner allows the counter-cut rows to fit together or "lock" because the seams lie in the opposite direction to the seams of the next row. Since the rows "lock" together, matching seams is quick and easy.

After each section has been sewn together, all the new seams will be pressed either to the left or to the right. In general, the seams of the Top and Bottom Sections are pressed to the right. The seams of the Center Section and Extra Top Section (if included) are pressed to the left. This pressing procedure will prepare the seam junctions to "lock" with those of the adjacent section when the quilt top is assembled.

> **Hint**
>
> *Find a large work area or floor space where the rows can be laid out in order as they are opened. Lay out about a third of the rows for the section and then start sewing them together. I find that if I try to lay out all the rows at once, invariably someone wants to use the table or floor space before the rows are sewn together.*

Figure 13 When counter-cuts are sewn together, the seam junctions should match up and "lock"

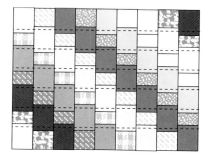

Begin assembling the Basic size quilt top by sorting the counter-cuts in the groups you will need for each section of the quilt. The chart below shows the counter-cut widths that are needed for the Top, Center, and Bottom sections of the Basic size. The letters along the top of the chart designate the counter-cut width, and correspond with those on the Basic Layout Plan. The Basic Layout Plan is located on pages 54–55.

Basic Size Counter-Cuts

Counter-Cut Letter	A	B	C	D	E
Counter-Cut Width	1½"	2"	2½"	3"	3½"
Number Used In Top Section	23	4	4	4	2
Number Used In Center Section	15	4	4	4	2
Number Used In Bottom Section	23	4	4	4	2
Total	61	12	12	12	6

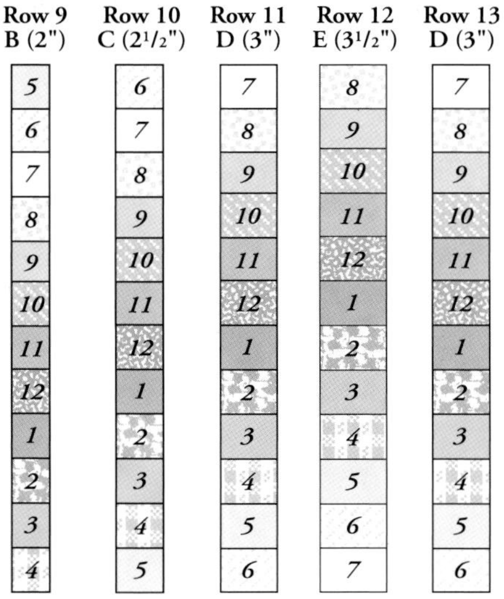

Assemble the sections in the order they are described on the following pages: the Top and Bottom Sections first and second, then the Center Section. The Center Section is completed last so that unused parts from other sections can be used for the "puzzle-pieced" rows.

◗ Basic Top Section

Row 1 of the Top Section starts on the left side with an **A** (1½") counter-cut. Take the seam apart between fabrics #9 and #8, as shown in Figure 14. The top fabric in the row is #9, the second #10, and the third #11, then going in sequence to the last piece which is fabric #8.

Row 2 uses an **A** counter-cut with the seam taken apart between fabrics #10 and #9. Fabric #10 is on top, followed by fabric #11 and so on, in sequence, to the last fabric #9. Row 3 again uses an **A** counter-cut with the seam taken apart between fabric #11 and fabric #10. Fabric #11 is on top, followed by fabric #12 and so on, in sequence, to fabric #10. Continue laying out the rows.

Note that row 9 changes to a **B** counter-cut. Row 10 uses a **C**, row 11 uses a **D**, and row 12 uses an **E**, which is the widest counter-cut. Row 13 goes back to a **D** counter-cut. Notice, too, that the flow of fabrics changes direction at this point. This is caused by selecting a different seam opening order in the counter-

Figure 14 Row 1 of Basic Top

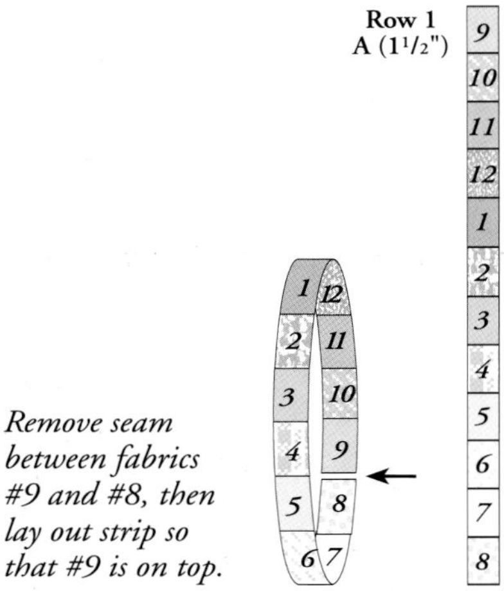

Row 1
A (1½")

Remove seam between fabrics #9 and #8, then lay out strip so that #9 is on top.

Row 1 A (1½"): 9, 10, 11, 12, 1, 2, 3, 4, 5, 6, 7, 8

Figure 15 Rows 9–13 of Basic Top

Row 9 B (2")	Row 10 C (2½")	Row 11 D (3")	Row 12 E (3½")	Row 13 D (3")
5	6	7	8	7
6	7	8	9	8
7	8	9	10	9
8	9	10	11	10
9	10	11	12	11
10	11	12	1	12
11	12	1	2	1
12	1	2	3	2
1	2	3	4	3
2	3	4	5	4
3	4	5	6	5
4	5	6	7	6

cut tube. When a seam is opened in a different sequence from the previous row, the fabric flows in a different direction. The design is now curving down over the first hump of the heart into the center.

When all rows are sewn together for the Top Section, press the seams to the right.

▼ Basic Bottom Section

The Bottom Section of the quilt is constructed in much the same manner as the Top Section. The main difference is that the fabrics flow in reverse sequence of the Top Section. Row 1 begins on the left side with fabric #1 at the top, followed by #12 and #11, and continues in sequence to the last fabric, #2. Row 2 will have fabric #12 on top followed by #11, #10, and so on, with fabric #1 being last. (This reverse fabric flow forms the bottom point of the heart.) After row #19, the center row, the flow of fabrics changes direction, now moving up to complete the lower right side of the heart. The flow of fabrics changes simply by changing the seam opening order.

Continue following the Layout Plan to complete the layout of the Bottom Section. When all rows are sewn together, press the seams to the right.

▼ Basic Center Section

The Center Section uses only 6 fabrics of each counter-cut unit per row. Start by laying out rows 1–13. Save the remaining halves of the units; they will be used to complete other rows. For example, the leftover segment from row 1 is used for row 7 (Figure 17) and the leftover part of row 2 is used for row 8.

After laying out and sewing together rows 1–13, skip over to the three center rows: 18,19, and 20. These three rows each use an **A** strip. Take the counter-cuts apart at the appropriate seams and sew these three rows together.

Skip to rows 25–37. Lay out the rows as illustrated on the Layout Plan. The leftover strip part from row 30 is used for row 36, and the leftover part from row 31 is used to make row 37. Sew rows 25–37 together.

About Puzzle-Pieced Rows: Rows 14–17 and 21–24 are constructed in a different manner. These are what I call "puzzle-pieced" rows, because they cannot be made up of single counter-cuts, but are pieced together with leftover parts of other rows. This is why puzzle-pieced rows are done last.

Rows 14–17 and rows 21–24 have some fabrics that appear twice in the same row. This creates the symmetrical band of color surrounding the #7 (center V) fabric. If there is a leftover part from a wider row that can be used, trim it to the narrower width. The first fabric in row 14 is #6, a leftover piece from row 10. For the rest of the row use a **C** unit. Open the appropriate seams, and use the section from fabric #7 down to fabric #3. Sew this segment to the #6 fabric, with #6 on top of #7.

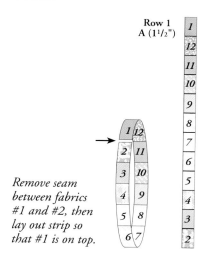

Figure 16 Row 1 of the Basic Bottom

Remove seam between fabrics #1 and #2, then lay out strip so that #1 is on top.

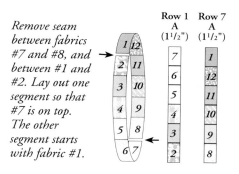

Figure 17 Rows 1 and 7 of the Basic Center

Remove seam between fabrics #7 and #8, and between #1 and #2. Lay out one segment so that #7 is on top. The other segment starts with fabric #1.

BASIC SIZE LAYOUT PLAN

Chapter 7 · 54

Top Section

Counter-cut strip:	I - - - A - - - - I B	C	D	E	D	C	B I - - - A - - - I B	C	D	E	D	C	B I - - - A - - - - I

Rows:	1	2	3	4	5	6	7	8	9	10	11	12	13	14	15	16	17	18	19	20	21	22	23	24	25	26	27	28	29	30	31	32	33	34	35	36	37
	9	10	11	12		2	3	4	5		7	8	7		5	4	3	2		2	3	4	5		7	8	7		5	4	3	2		12	11	10	9
	10	11	12		2	3	4	5		7	8		9	8	7		5	4	3	2	3	4	5		7	8		9	8	7		5	4	3	2		12	11	10
	11	12		2	3	4	5		7	8		9		10	9	8	7		5	4	3	4	5		7	8		9		10	9	8	7		5	4	3	2		12	11
	12		2	3	4	5		7	8	9		10	11	10		9	8	7		5	4	5		7	8	9		10	11	10		9	8	7		5	4	3	2		12
		2	3	4	5		7	8	9		10	11		12	11	10	9	8	7		5		7	8	9		10	11		12	11	10	9	8	7		5	4	3	2
	2	3	4	5		7	8	9	10	11		12		12	11	10	9	8	7		7	8	9	10	11		12		12	11	10	9	8	7		5	4	3	2
	3	4	5		7	8	9	10	11		12		2		12	11	10	9	8	7	8	9	10	11		12		2		12	11	10	9	8	7		5	4	3
	4	5		7	8	9	10	11	12		2		3		2		12	11	10	9	8	9	10	11	12		2		3		2		12	11	10	9	8	7		5	4
	5		7	8	9	10	11	12		2	3	4		3	2		12	11	10	9	10	11	12		2	3	4		3	2		12	11	10	9	8	7		5
		7	8	9	10	11	12		2	3	4	5	4	3	2		12	11	10	11	12		2	3	4	5		4	3	2		12	11	10	9	8	7
	7	8	9	10	11	12		2	3	4	5		5	4	3	2		12	11	12		2	3	4	5		5	4	3	2		12	11	10	9	8	7
	8	9	10	11	12		2	3	4	5		7		5	4	3	2		12		2	3	4	5		7		5	4	3	2		12	11	10	9	8

Center Section

Bottom Section

Rows: (Center Section columns) 1 2 3 4 5 6 7 8 9 10 11 12 13 14 15 16 17 18 19 20 21 22 23 24 25 26 27 28 29 30 31 32 33 34 35 36 37

Counter-cut strip: I – – – A – – – I B   C   D   E   D   C   B I – – – A – – – I B   C   D   E   D   C   B I – – – A – – – I

Rows: (Bottom Section columns) 1 2 3 4 5 6 7 8 9 10 11 12 13 14 15 16 17 18 19 20 21 22 23 24 25 26 27 28 29 30 31 32 33 34 35 36 37

Figure 18 Row 15 of Basic Center

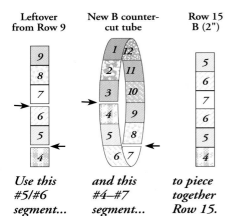

Leftover from Row 9

New B counter-cut tube

Row 15 B (2")

Use this #5/#6 segment...

and this #4–#7 segment...

to piece together Row 15.

Figure 19 Sewing sections together

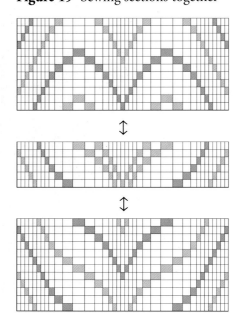

Row 15 starts with a unit made up of fabrics #5 and #6, left over from row 9. Take a new **B** counter-cut and open the seams between fabrics #3 and #4, and fabrics #7 and #8. Use the segment of the counter-cut from fabric #7 down through fabric # 4. Sew this part to the #5/#6 piece to complete the row.

Rows 16, 17, 21, and 22 are also puzzle-pieced rows. If you have any strata tube left, you may want to cut new counter-cuts for these rows rather than piecing them together with scraps.

Row 23 starts with the #5/#6 unit left over from row 29, with the appropriate section from a **B** strip added on to it. Follow the Layout Plan carefully for the correct fabric sequences. Row 24 uses the leftover fabric #6 from row 28 and a section of a **C** counter-cut for the rest of the row.

When all the rows are sewn together for the Center Section, press the seams to the left. This is the opposite direction from the Top and Bottom Sections.

Completing the Heart Design

Sew the Top, Center, and Bottom Sections together. The seams will lock together since the seams of the sections were pressed in opposing directions. The quilt top is now complete and ready for borders to be added. Borders for all quilt sizes are discussed in Chapter 11.

8

Version 1 Heart Construction

This chapter provides specific layout instructions for the Version 1 Quilts—the Twin, Full, and Queen sizes. These quilt sizes are grouped together because they are all made with 2½" wide strips, and all use the same range of counter-cut widths.

Before assembling any of the quilts in this chapter, be sure to read the first half of Chapter 7, "Basic Heart Construction." It contains information about the specific construction techniques, such as sewing and pressing, needed to assemble the Bargello Heart design.

The Twin size quilt is constructed in the same manner as the Basic size, discussed in Chapter 7. However, there are differences. Some rows have been removed on each side of the quilt top, and there is an Extra Top Section added, creating enough length for a bed. The extra section is added only to the top of the heart image so that the heart stays centered on the bed. The additional rows will go over or under the pillow.

Begin by sorting the counter-cuts into the groups to be used for the Extra Top, Top, Center, and Bottom Sections. The chart below shows the size and the number of counter-cuts needed for all sections of the heart. The letters along the top of the chart designate counter-cut width, and correspond with those on the Twin Size Layout Plan.

Twin Size Counter-Cuts

Counter-Cut Letter	A	B	C	D	E
Counter-Cut Width	1½"	2"	2½"	3"	3½"
Number used for Extra Top Section	17	4	4	4	2
Number used for Top Section	17	4	4	4	2
Number used for Center Section	10	4	4	4	2
Number used for Bottom Section	17	4	4	4	2
Total	61	16	16	16	8

Assemble the sections in the order they are described on the following pages: the Top and Bottom Sections first and second, then the Extra Top Section, and finally the Center Section. The Center Section is completed last so that unused parts from other sections can be used for the "puzzle-pieced" rows. Refer to the Twin Size Layout Plan, on pages 60–61, as you follow the layout instructions for each section.

Twin Top Section

Row 1 begins on the left side with an **A** counter-cut. Take the seam apart between fabrics #11 and #12. Have your Fabric Chart and Layout Plan close at hand for easy reference. The top fabric of row 1 is #12. Fabric #1 is second, #2 third, and so on down to the last fabric, which is #11.

Row 2 uses an **A** counter-cut with the seam opened between fabrics #1 and #12. The first fabric is #1, followed by #2, and so on down to fabric #12. Continue laying out the rows for the Top Section. Watch for the rows where the counter-cut width and/or fabric direction changes.

When all 31 rows of the Twin Top Section have been sewn together, press the seams to the right.

 ## Twin Bottom Section

Row 1 of the Bottom Section also starts with an **A** counter-cut. Open the seam between fabrics #4 and #5. Fabric #4 is the top fabric of the row, followed by #3, and continuing in sequence to fabric #5 at the bottom. The flow of the fabrics is in reverse order to that of the Top Section. Referring to the Layout Plan, continue laying out and sewing together the rows of the Bottom Section. Press this section with the seams going to the right.

 ## Twin Extra Top Section

This section uses eight fabrics of each counter-cut unit per row. The rows in this section are laid out in the same way as the Top and Bottom Sections. The only difference is that four fabric pieces of the counter-cut are not used. By making the Extra Top Section before the Center Section, the leftover portions can be utilized in the "puzzle-pieced" rows in the Center Section.

As shown on the Twin Size Layout Plan, row 1 begins with fabric #4 and ends with fabric #11. Take the seams apart between fabrics #3 and #4, and fabrics #11 and #12. Remove the leftover segment and reserve it for later use.

When all the rows are sewn together, press the seams toward the left.

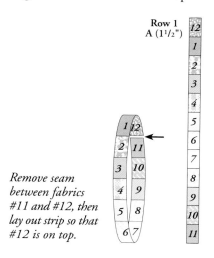

Figure 20 Row 1 of Twin Top

Remove seam between fabrics #11 and #12, then lay out strip so that #12 is on top.

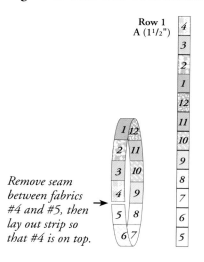

Figure 21 Row 1 of Twin Bottom

Remove seam between fabrics #4 and #5, then lay out strip so that #4 is on top.

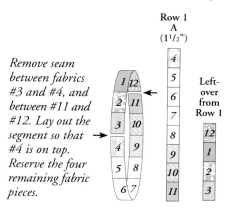

Figure 22 Row 1 of Twin Extra Top

Remove seam between fabrics #3 and #4, and between #11 and #12. Lay out the segment so that #4 is on top. Reserve the four remaining fabric pieces.

TWIN SIZE LAYOUT PLAN

Extra Top Section

Top Section

Counter-cut strip: 1 - - A - - 1B C D E D - - 1B - - A - - 1B C D E D C B1 - - A - 1

Rows: 1 2 3 4 5 6 7 8 9 10 11 12 13 14 15 16 17 18 19 20 21 22 23 24 25 26 27 28 29 30 31

Center Section

Bottom Section

Counter-cut strip:

Rows:

Figure 23 Rows 3 and 16 of Twin Center

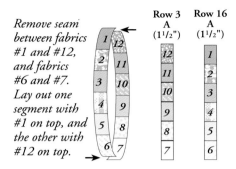

Remove seam between fabrics #1 and #12, and fabrics #6 and #7. Lay out one segment with #1 on top, and the other with #12 on top.

Figure 24 Sewing sections together

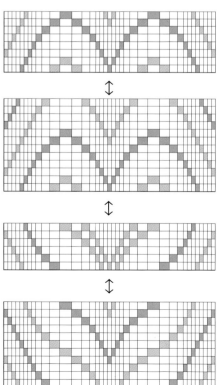

Twin Center Section

The Center Section uses only six fabrics—half of a counter-cut unit—for each row. Save the unused portions; some will be used for other rows or parts of rows. Lay out rows 1–10, separating the seams at the appropriate places. (The leftover segments from rows 3 and 4 will be used for rows 16 and 15.) Sew rows 1–10 together.

Rows 11–14 and 18–21 use fabric #6, and some others, twice in the same row. This forms the symmetrical band of color surrounding fabric #7 at the center of the heart. These are the "puzzle-pieced" rows and should be done last.

Skip to the three center rows, 15, 16, and 17. Rows 15 and 16 use leftover segments from rows 3 and 4. The extra segment from row 17 is set aside and used for row 28. Sew the three center rows together.

Continue by laying out and sewing together rows 22–31.

Now go back to the "puzzle-pieced" rows, 11–14 and 18–21. These rows are all pieced together from leftovers. Row 11 starts with fabric #6, left over from row 7, with the remaining fabrics coming from a **C** counter-cut. Row 12 starts with a unit made up of fabrics #5 and #6 (left over from row 6) and is completed with a section of fabrics from a **B** counter-cut. Use any appropriate leftover pieces to complete rows 13, 14, 18, and 19. Lay out and sew together rows 20 and 21 following the Layout Plan.

Sew all the rows together and press the seams to the left.

Completing the Heart Design

Now you are ready to sew the four sections, Extra Top, Top, Center, and Bottom, together. If you followed the pressing instructions, the seam junctions of each section should "lock" together. The Twin size heart design is now ready for the borders. Borders for all sizes are discussed in Chapter 11.

FULL SIZE — 53" x 76"

The Full size quilt is constructed in the same manner as the Basic size, discussed in Chapter 7. Begin by sorting the counter-cuts into the groups to be used for the Extra Top, Top, Center, and Bottom Sections. The chart below shows the size and the number of counter-cuts needed for all sections of the heart. The letters along the top of the chart designate counter-cut widths, and correspond with those on the Full Size Layout Plan, located on the following two pages.

Full Size Counter-Cuts

Counter-Cut Letter	A	B	C	D	E
Counter-Cut Width	1½"	2"	2½"	3"	3½"
Number used for Extra Top Section	23	4	4	4	2
Number used for Top Section	23	4	4	4	2
Number used for Center Section	14	4	4	4	2
Number used for Bottom Section	23	4	4	4	2
Total	83	16	16	16	8

Assemble the sections in the order they are described on the following pages: the Top and Bottom Sections first and second, then the Extra Top Section, and finally the Center Section. The Center Section is completed last so that unused parts from other sections can be used for the "puzzle-pieced" rows. For example, four fabrics from each counter-cut of the Extra Top Section are not needed, and can be used to piece the Center Section. Refer to the Full Size Layout Plan as you follow the layout instructions for each section.

FULL SIZE LAYOUT PLAN

Extra Top Section

Top Section

Counter-
cut strip:

Rows:

Center Section

Bottom Section

Counter-cut strip:

Rows:

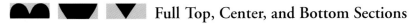 **Full Top, Center, and Bottom Sections**

These sections are all made exactly like the Basic size. The number of rows, the fabric placement, and the counter-cut seam separations are identical. Follow the Basic Size instructions in Chapter 7 to assemble these sections. (The Full Size Layout Plan is on the previous two pages.)

Full Extra Top Section

Eight fabrics are used in each row of the Extra Top. Four fabrics are left over from the counter-cuts after the seams are separated. Start with an **A** counter-cut for row 1 and open the seam between fabrics #1 and #12. Fabrics #1 through #8 are used for this row, so remove fabrics #9 through #12. Refer to the Full Size Layout Plan for the fabric sequence of this section. Remember to remove the four extra fabric pieces from each counter-cut. When all the rows are laid out and sewn together, press the seams toward the left.

Completing the Heart Design

Now you are ready to sew the four sections, Extra Top, Top, Center, and Bottom, together. If you followed the pressing instructions, the seam junctions of each section should "lock" together. The Full size heart design is now ready for the borders. Borders for all sizes are discussed in Chapter 11.

Figure 25 Row 1 of Full Extra Top

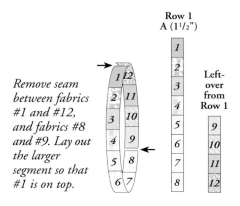

Remove seam between fabrics #1 and #12, and fabrics #8 and #9. Lay out the larger segment so that #1 is on top.

Figure 26 Sewing sections together

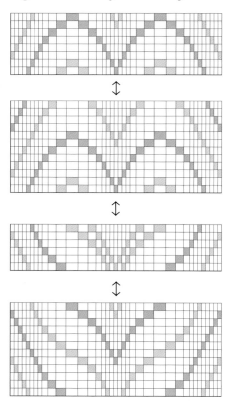

QUEEN SIZE — 60" x 80"

The Queen size quilt is constructed in the same manner as the Basic size, discussed in Chapter 7. The Queen size is slightly wider and longer than the Basic size. Four rows are added to each side, and an Extra Top Section makes it long enough to fit a Queen size bed.

Begin by sorting the counter-cuts into the groups to be used for the Extra Top, Top, Center, and Bottom Sections. The chart below shows the size and the number of counter-cuts needed for all sections of the heart. The letters along the top of the chart designate counter-cut width and correspond with those on the Queen Size Layout Plan, located on the following two pages.

Queen Size Counter-Cuts

Counter-Cut Letter	A	B	C	D	E
Counter-Cut Width	1½"	2"	2½"	3"	3½"
Number used for Extra Top Section	31	4	4	4	2
Number used for Top Section	31	4	4	4	2
Number used for Center Section	15	4	4	4	2
Number used for Bottom Section	31	4	4	4	2
Total	108	16	16	16	8

Assemble the sections in the order they are described on the following pages: the Top and Bottom Sections first and second, then the Extra Top Section, and finally the Center Section. The Center Section is completed last so that unused parts from other sections can be used for the "puzzle-pieced" rows. Refer to the Queen Size Layout Plan as you follow the layout instructions for each section.

 Queen Top Section

Row 1 starts on the left with an **A** counter-cut. Open the seam between fabrics #5 and #4. Fabric #5 is in the top position and fabric #4 at the bottom. The first 12 rows all use an **A** counter-cut. At row 13 the counter-cuts start changing widths. Carefully follow the Queen Size Layout Plan for all width and fabric order changes. When all rows are sewn together, press the seams to the right.

Figure 27 Row 1 of Queen Top

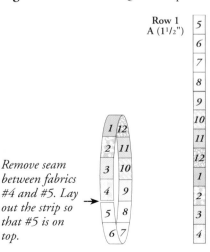

Remove seam between fabrics #4 and #5. Lay out the strip so that #5 is on top.

QUEEN SIZE LAYOUT PLAN

Extra Top Section

Top Section

Counter-cut strip: | - - - A - - - | B | C | D | E | D | C | B | - - - A - - - | B | C | D | E | D | C | B | - - - A - - - |

Rows: 1 2 3 4 5 6 7 8 9 10 11 12 13 14 15 16 17 18 19 20 21 22 23 24 25 26 27 28 29 30 31 32 33 34 35 36 37 38 39 40 41 42 43 44 45

Center Section

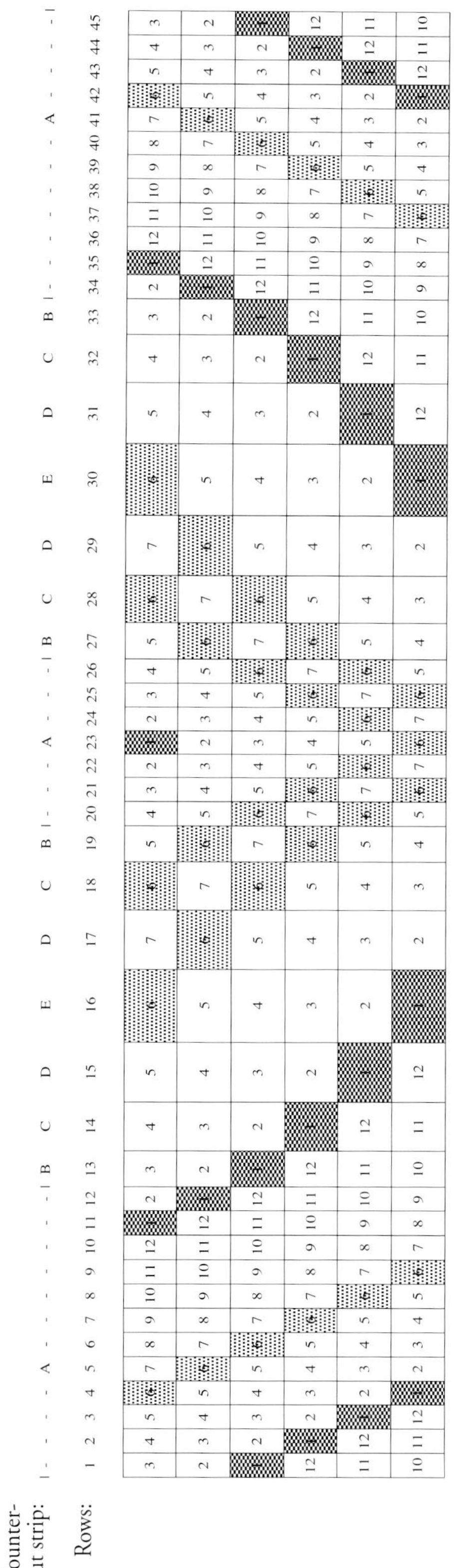

Bottom Section

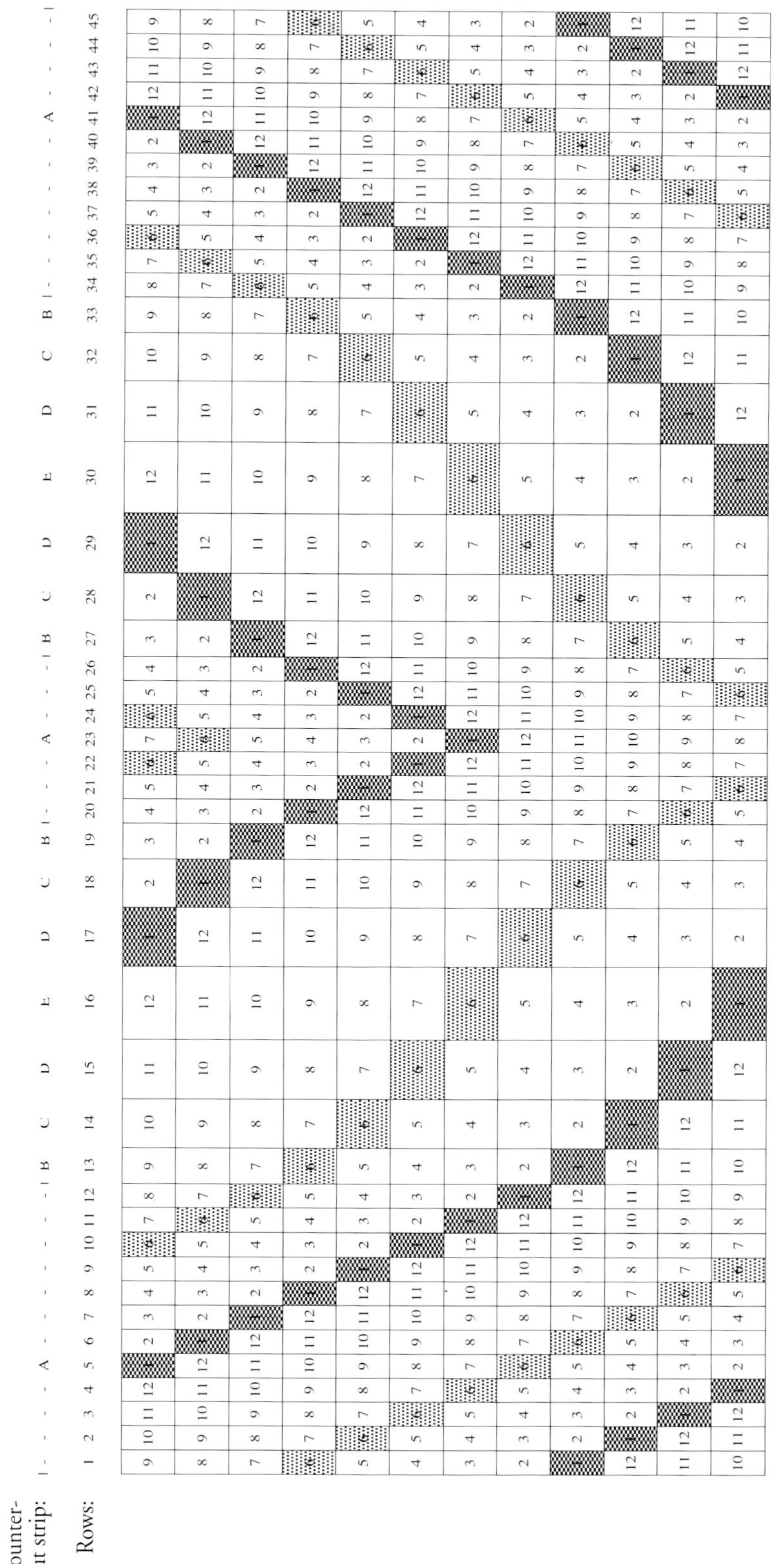

▼ Queen Bottom Section

The Bottom Section is constructed in much the same manner as the Top Section except that the fabrics flow in the opposite direction. Refer to the Layout Plan for the row layout of the Bottom Section. When all the rows are sewn together, press the seams toward the right.

● Queen Extra Top Section

The Extra Top Section uses ten fabrics from each counter-cut. The rows are laid out in the same way as the Top and Bottom, except two fabrics are removed as each tubed unit is opened. The two pieces removed from the counter-cuts can be utilized later in the Center Section. Start with row 1. Fabric #7 is at the top and fabric #4 at the bottom. Continue to lay out the rows following the Layout Plan. Sew all the rows together and press the seams to the left.

▼ Queen Center Section

The Center Section rows use only six fabrics from each counter-cut. Most of the remaining parts are used in other rows. Start by laying out rows 1–12. The leftover halves from rows 1–6 are used to make rows 7–12. Next, lay out rows 13–17.

Skip to the center rows, 22, 23, and 24. Using **A** counter-cuts, open the seams at the appropriate places and lay them out in order. Sew the three center rows together. Lay out and sew together rows 28–33, then rows 34–39. For rows 40–45, use the leftover parts of rows 34–39. After laying out these rows, sew them together.

Rows 18–21 and 25–28 are the "puzzle-pieced" rows, and are made by combining leftover parts from other rows. Some fabrics are used twice in the same row to form the center of the heart. Wider leftover pieces from the Center and Extra Top sections can be cut narrower to piece together some of these rows.

When all the rows are prepared and sewn together, press the seam allowances to the left.

Completing the Heart Design

Now you are ready to sew the four sections, Extra Top, Top, Center, and Bottom, together. If you followed the pressing instructions, the seam junctions of each section should "lock" together. The Queen size heart design is now ready for the borders. Borders for all sizes are discussed in Chapter 11.

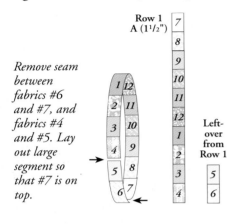

Figure 28 Row 1 of Queen Top

Remove seam between fabrics #6 and #7, and fabrics #4 and #5. Lay out large segment so that #7 is on top.

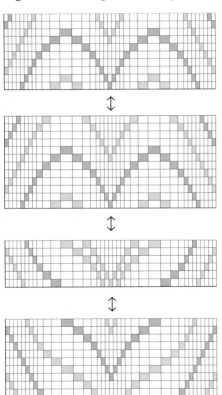

Figure 29 Sewing sections together

9
Version 2 Heart Construction

This chapter provides specific layout instructions for the Version 2 Quilts—the Mini, Baby, and King sizes. These additional quilt sizes are achieved by changing the fabric strip width in the strata unit, and using different counter-cut widths.

Before assembling any of the quilts in this chapter, be sure to read the first half of Chapter 7, "Basic Heart Construction." It contains information about the specific construction techniques, such as sewing and pressing, needed to assemble the Bargello Heart.

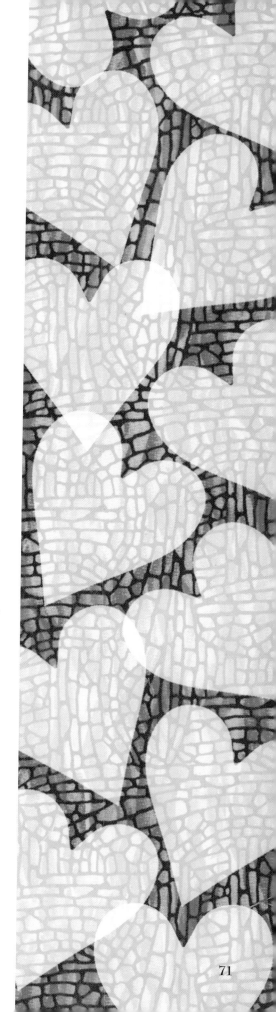

The Mini size quilt is constructed in the same manner as the Basic size, discussed in Chapter 7. However, the fabric strips used to create its strata units are cut only 1½" wide. Also, the Mini size quilt uses smaller counter-cut widths.

Begin by sorting the counter-cuts into the groups to be used for the Top, Center, and Bottom Sections. The chart below shows the size and the number of counter-cuts needed for all sections of the heart. The letters along the top of the chart designate the counter-cut widths, and correspond with those on the Mini Size Layout Plan, located on pages 74–75.

Mini Size Counter-Cuts

Counter-Cut Letter	A	B	C	D	E
Counter-Cut Width	¾"	1"	1½"	2"	2½"
Number used for Top Section	23	4	4	4	2
Number used for Center Section	15	4	4	4	2
Number used for Bottom Section	23	4	4	4	2
Total	61	12	12	12	6

Assemble the sections in the order they are described on the next page: the Top and Bottom Sections first and second, then the Center Section. The Center Section is completed last so that unused parts from other sections can be used for the "puzzle-pieced" rows. Refer to the Mini Size Layout Plan as you follow the layout instructions for each section.

Mini Top, Center, and Bottom Sections

The sections of the Mini size are made exactly like the Basic size. The number of rows, fabric placement, and the counter-cut seam separations are identical. Follow the Basic Size instructions in Chapter 7 to assemble the sections. The Mini Size Layout Plan is located on the next two pages.

Completing the Heart Design

Now you are ready to sew the three sections—Top, Center, and Bottom—together. If you followed the pressing instructions, the seams of each section should "lock" together. The Mini size heart design is now ready for the borders. Borders for all sizes are discussed in Chapter 11.

Figure 30 Sewing sections together

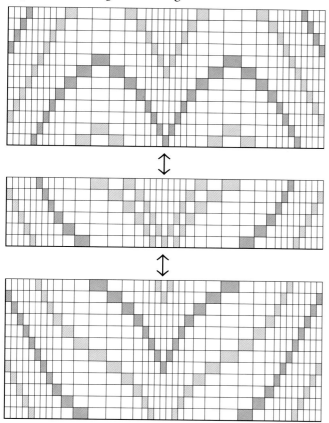

MINI SIZE LAYOUT PLAN

Top Section

Counter-cut strip: I - - - A - - - I B C D E D C B I - - - A - - - I B C D E D C B I - - - A - - - I

Rows: 1 2 3 4 5 6 7 8 9 10 11 12 13 14 15 16 17 18 19 20 21 22 23 24 25 26 27 28 29 30 31 32 33 34 35 36 37

Center Section

Bottom Section

Rows:

Counter-cut strip:

Rows:

The Baby size quilt is constructed in the same manner as the Basic size, discussed in Chapter 7. However, the fabric strips used to create its strata units are cut only 2" wide. Also, the Baby size quilt uses smaller counter-cut widths.

Begin by sorting the counter-cuts into the groups to be used for the Top, Center, and Bottom Sections. The chart below shows the size and the number of counter-cuts needed for all sections of the heart. The letters along the top of the chart designate the counter-cut widths, and correspond with those on the Baby Size Layout Plan, located on pages 78–79.

Baby Size Counter-Cuts

Counter-Cut Letter	A	B	C	D	E
Counter-Cut Width	1"	1½"	2"	2½"	3"
Number used for Top Section	23	4	4	4	2
Number used for Center Section	15	4	4	4	2
Number used for Bottom Section	23	4	4	4	2
Total	61	12	12	12	6

Assemble the sections in the order they are described on the next page: the Top and Bottom Sections first and second, then the Center Section. The Center Section is completed last so that unused parts from other sections can be used for the "puzzle-pieced" rows. Refer to the Baby Size Layout Plan as you follow the layout instructions for each section.

Baby Top, Center, and Bottom Sections

These sections are all made exactly like the Basic size. The number of rows, fabric placement, and counter-cut seam separations are identical. Follow the Basic Size instructions in Chapter 7 to assemble these sections. The Baby Size Layout Plan is on the next two pages.

Completing the Heart Design

Now you are ready to sew the three sections—Top, Center, and Bottom—together. If you followed the pressing instructions, the seams of each section should "lock" together. The Baby size heart design is now ready for the borders. Borders for all sizes are discussed in Chapter 11.

Figure 31 Sewing sections together

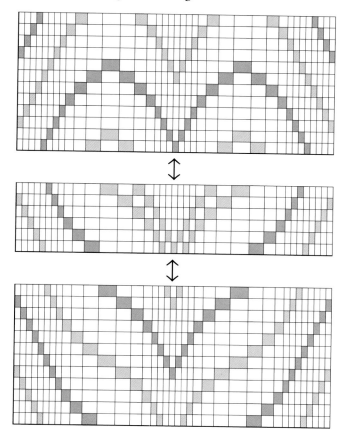

BABY SIZE LAYOUT PLAN

Top Section

Counter-cut strip:

Rows:

Center Section

Bottom Section

Rows:

Counter-cut strip:

Rows:

Version 2 Heart Construction ❧ 79

The King size quilt is constructed in the same manner as the Basic size, discussed in Chapter 7. However, the fabric strips used to create its strata units are cut 3" wide. Also, the King size quilt uses larger counter-cut widths.

Begin by sorting the counter-cuts into the groups to be used for the Extra Top, Top, Center, and Bottom Sections. The chart below shows the size and the number of counter-cuts needed for all sections of the heart. The letters along the top of the chart designate the counter-cut widths and correspond with those on the King Size Layout Plan, which is located on pages 82–83.

King Size Counter-Cuts

Counter-Cut Letter	A	B	C	D	E
Counter-Cut Width	2"	2½"	3"	3½"	4"
Number used for Extra Top Section	*	*	*	*	*
Number used for Top Section	29	4	4	4	2
Number used for Center Section	17	4	4	4	2
Number used for Bottom Section	29	4	4	4	2
Total	75	12	12	12	6

Since the Extra Top Section uses only two fabrics in each row, the counter-cut rows are made from leftover pieces from the Center Section or cut from leftover fabrics.

Assemble the sections in the order they are described on the next page: the Top and Bottom Sections first and second, then the Center, and finally the Extra Top Sections. The Center and Extra Top Sections are completed last so that unused parts from other sections can be used to piece them. Refer to the King Size Layout Plan as you follow the layout instructions for each section.

King Top Section

Follow the Layout Plan on the following two pages for the row layout. Row 1 starts on the left with an **A** counter-cut. Open the seam between fabrics #6 and #5. Fabric #6 is the top fabric, followed in sequence to the bottom fabric, #5. The first 11 rows use **A** counter-cuts. Row 12 changes to a **B** counter-cut. Refer to the Layout Plan for the other row width and color flow changes. After all of the rows have been laid out and sewn together, press the seams to the right.

 King Bottom Section

The Bottom Section is constructed in the same manner as the Top Section. The fabric flow is in the opposite order so that the point of the heart is formed. This change in direction is created by opening the counter-cut seams in reverse order. Row 1 starts with fabric #10 on top and ends with fabric #11. Refer to the Layout Plan and continue the row layout for the Bottom Section. When all the rows have been laid out and sewn together, iron the seams to the right.

 King Center Section

The rows in the Center Section use six fabrics from each counter-cut. The remaining parts of rows 1–5 are used for rows 7–11. The leftovers from rows 33–37 make rows 39–43. Lay out and sew these two sections first.

About Puzzle-Pieced Rows: Rows 17–20 and 24–27 are constructed in a different manner. These are what I call "puzzle-pieced" rows, because they cannot be made up of single counter-cuts, but are pieced together with leftover parts of other rows. The puzzle-pieced rows are done last for this reason.

Rows 17–20 and 24–27 have some fabrics that appear twice in the same row. This creates the symmetrical band of color surrounding the #7 (center V) fabric. If there is a leftover part from a wider row that can be used, trim it to the narrower width. The first fabric in row 17 is #6, a leftover piece from row 13. For the rest of the row use part of a **C** counter-cut. Open the appropriate seams, and use the section of the tube from fabric #7 to fabric #3. Sew this segment to the #6 fabric, with #6 on top of #7.

Continue to assemble and lay out the the puzzle-pieced rows in this manner. Sew them together, and then sew all the row sections together to form the Center Section. Press the seams to the left.

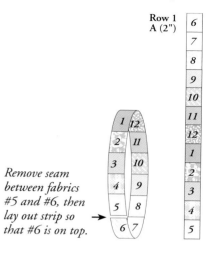

Figure 32 Row 1 of King Top

Remove seam between fabrics #5 and #6, then lay out strip so that #6 is on top.

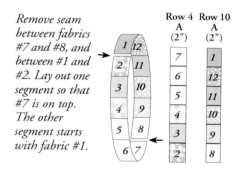

Figure 33 Rows 4 and 10 of King Center

Remove seam between fabrics #7 and #8, and between #1 and #2. Lay out one segment so that #7 is on top. The other segment starts with fabric #1.

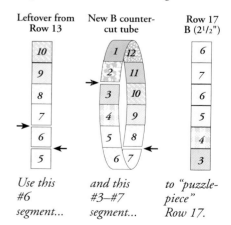

Figure 34 Row 17 of King Center

Use this #6 segment... *and this #3–#7 segment...* *to "puzzle-piece" Row 17.*

KING SIZE LAYOUT PLAN

Extra Top Section

Top Section

Counter-cut strip: 1 - - - - A - - - - - 1B   C   D   E   D   C   1B - - - A - - - - 1B   C   D   E   D   C   B1 - - - A - - - - A - - - - 1

Rows: 1 2 3 4 5 6 7 8 9 10 11 12 13 14 15 16 17 18 19 20 21 22 23 24 25 26 27 28 29 30 31 32 33 34 35 36 37 38 39 40 41 42 43

Center Section

Counter-cut strip:	A	A	A	A	A	A	A	A	A	A	A	B	C	D	E	D	C	B	A	A	A	A	A	A	A	B	C	D	E	D	C	B	A	A	A	A	A	A	A	A	A	A	A
Rows:	1	2	3	4	5	6	7	8	9	10	11	12	13	14	15	16	17	18	19	20	21	22	23	24	25	26	27	28	29	30	31	32	33	34	35	36	37	38	39	40	41	42	43
	4	5	6	7	8	9	10	11	12	1	2	3	4	5	6	7	6	5	4	3	2	1	2	3	4	5	6	7	6	5	4	3	2	1	12	11	10	9	8	7	6	5	4
	3	4	5	6	7	8	9	10	11	12	1	2	3	4	5	6	7	6	5	4	3	2	3	4	5	6	7	6	5	4	3	2	1	12	11	10	9	8	7	6	5	4	3
	2	3	4	5	6	7	8	9	10	11	12	1	2	3	4	5	6	7	6	5	4	3	4	5	6	7	6	5	4	3	2	1	12	11	10	9	8	7	6	5	4	3	2
	1	2	3	4	5	6	7	8	9	10	11	12	1	2	3	4	5	6	7	6	5	4	5	6	7	6	5	4	3	2	1	12	11	10	9	8	7	6	5	4	3	2	1
	12	1	2	3	4	5	6	7	8	9	10	11	12	1	2	3	4	5	6	7	6	5	6	7	6	5	4	3	2	1	12	11	10	9	8	7	6	5	4	3	2	1	12
	11	12	1	2	3	4	5	6	7	8	9	10	11	12	1	2	3	4	5	6	7	6	7	6	5	4	3	2	1	12	11	10	9	8	7	6	5	4	3	2	1	12	11

Bottom Section

Counter-cut strip:	A	A	A	A	A	A	A	A	A	A	A	B	C	D	E	D	C	B	A	A	A	A	A	A	A	B	C	D	E	D	C	B	A	A	A	A	A	A	A	A	A	A	A
Rows:	1	2	3	4	5	6	7	8	9	10	11	12	13	14	15	16	17	18	19	20	21	22	23	24	25	26	27	28	29	30	31	32	33	34	35	36	37	38	39	40	41	42	43
	10	11	12	1	2	3	4	5	6	7	8	9	10	11	12	1	2	3	4	5	6	7	6	5	4	3	2	1	12	11	10	9	8	7	6	5	4	3	2	1	12	11	10
	9	10	11	12	1	2	3	4	5	6	7	8	9	10	11	12	1	2	3	4	5	6	5	4	3	2	1	12	11	10	9	8	7	6	5	4	3	2	1	12	11	10	9
	8	9	10	11	12	1	2	3	4	5	6	7	8	9	10	11	12	1	2	3	4	5	4	3	2	1	12	11	10	9	8	7	6	5	4	3	2	1	12	11	10	9	8
	7	8	9	10	11	12	1	2	3	4	5	6	7	8	9	10	11	12	1	2	3	4	3	2	1	12	11	10	9	8	7	6	5	4	3	2	1	12	11	10	9	8	7
	6	7	8	9	10	11	12	1	2	3	4	5	6	7	8	9	10	11	12	1	2	3	2	1	12	11	10	9	8	7	6	5	4	3	2	1	12	11	10	9	8	7	6
	5	6	7	8	9	10	11	12	1	2	3	4	5	6	7	8	9	10	11	12	1	2	1	12	11	10	9	8	7	6	5	4	3	2	1	12	11	10	9	8	7	6	5
	4	5	6	7	8	9	10	11	12	1	2	3	4	5	6	7	8	9	10	11	12	1	12	11	10	9	8	7	6	5	4	3	2	1	12	11	10	9	8	7	6	5	4
	3	4	5	6	7	8	9	10	11	12	1	2	3	4	5	6	7	8	9	10	11	12	11	10	9	8	7	6	5	4	3	2	1	12	11	10	9	8	7	6	5	4	3
	2	3	4	5	6	7	8	9	10	11	12	1	2	3	4	5	6	7	8	9	10	11	10	9	8	7	6	5	4	3	2	1	12	11	10	9	8	7	6	5	4	3	2
	1	2	3	4	5	6	7	8	9	10	11	12	1	2	3	4	5	6	7	8	9	10	9	8	7	6	5	4	3	2	1	12	11	10	9	8	7	6	5	4	3	2	1
	12	1	2	3	4	5	6	7	8	9	10	11	12	1	2	3	4	5	6	7	8	9	8	7	6	5	4	3	2	1	12	11	10	9	8	7	6	5	4	3	2	1	12
	11	12	1	2	3	4	5	6	7	8	9	10	11	12	1	2	3	4	5	6	7	8	7	6	5	4	3	2	1	12	11	10	9	8	7	6	5	4	3	2	1	12	11

Figure 35 Individual piece sizes for King Extra Top

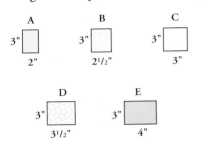

Figure 36 Sewing sections together

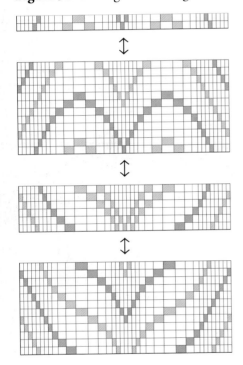

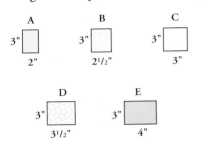 **King Extra Top Section**

Since each row needs only two fabrics, use leftover pieces from the Center Section. All other needed pieces are cut from the remaining fabric yardage. Sew the rows together and press the seams to the left.

Note: Any pieces cut from remaining yardage should measure 3" in height by the width of the row that they are needed for, as shown in Figure 35.

Completing the Heart Design

Now you are ready to sew the four sections, Extra Top, Top, Center, and Bottom, together. If you followed the pressing instructions, the seams of each section should "lock" together. The King size heart design is now ready for the borders. Borders for all sizes are discussed in Chapter 11.

10

Design Variations

In most of the Bargello Heart Quilts presented in this book, the colors radiate outward from the center of the quilt to the edges—from light to dark, then dark to light—in wide bands. This chapter shows two ways to alter this look: reversing the seam opening order to make diamonds appear at the top, and changing the color value order to emphasize different areas of the heart design.

EXTRA TOP VARIATIONS

One appealing variation is to change the color flow direction in the Extra Top Section of the Twin, Full, or Queen size quilts. With this change, the heart design stops radiating out and diamonds begin to appear. The Queen size quilt on page 48 in the "Bargello Heart Gallery" has been made using this variation.

There is no change in the number of counter-cuts. The variation is achieved simply by using a different seam opening order for the the Extra Top Section. Layout plans for the three Extra Top Variations are located on the next page. If you are making a Twin, Full, or Queen size quilt, use the appropriate Extra Top Variation instead of the regular Extra Top Section for that size.

Note: Because the King size Extra Top Section has only two rows of fabric, a change of fabric direction would not be apparent. Therefore there is no Extra Top Variation for this quilt size.

Twin Size Extra Top Variation

|- - -A- - -|B   C   D   E   D   C   B|- - - A - - -|B   C   D   E   D   C   B|- - -A- - -|

1 2 3 4 5 6   7   8   9   10   11   12 13 14 15 16 17 18 19 20   21   22   23   24   25   26 27 28 29 30 31

8	9	10	11	12	▓	2	3	4	3	2	▓	12	11	10	9	10	11	12	▓	2	3	4	3	2	▓	12	11	10	9	8
7	8	9	10	11	12	▓	2	3	2	▓	12	11	10	9	8	9	10	11	12	▓	2	3	2	▓	12	11	10	9	8	7
▓	7	8	9	10	11	12	▓	2	▓	12	11	10	9	8	7	8	9	10	11	12	▓	2	▓	12	11	10	9	8	7	▓
5	▓	7	8	9	10	11	12	▓	12	11	10	9	8	7	▓	7	8	9	10	11	12	▓	12	11	10	9	8	7	▓	5
4	5	▓	7	8	9	10	11	12	11	10	9	8	7	▓	5	▓	7	8	9	10	11	12	11	10	9	8	7	▓	5	4
3	4	5	▓	7	8	9	10	11	10	9	8	7	▓	5	4	5	▓	7	8	9	10	11	10	9	8	7	▓	5	4	3
2	3	4	5	▓	7	8	9	10	9	8	7	▓	5	4	3	4	5	▓	7	8	9	10	9	8	7	▓	5	4	3	2
▓	2	3	4	5	▓	7	8	9	8	7	▓	5	4	3	2	3	4	5	▓	7	8	9	8	7	▓	5	4	3	2	▓

Full Size Extra Top Variation

|- - -A- - -|B   C   D   E   D   C   B|- - - A - - -|B   C   D   E   D   C   B|- - - A - - -|

1 2 3 4 5 6 7 8 9   10   11   12   13   14   15 16 17 18 19 20 21 22 23   24   25   26   27   28   29 30 31 32 33 34 35 36 37

5	▓	7	8	9	10	11	12	▓	2	3	4	3	2	▓	12	11	10	9	10	11	12	▓	2	3	4	3	2	▓	12	11	10	9	8	7	▓	5
4	5	▓	7	8	9	10	11	12	▓	2	3	2	▓	12	11	10	9	8	9	10	11	12	▓	2	3	2	▓	12	11	10	9	8	7	▓	5	4
3	4	5	▓	7	8	9	10	11	12	▓	2	▓	12	11	10	9	8	7	8	9	10	11	12	▓	2	▓	12	11	10	9	8	7	▓	5	4	3
2	3	4	5	▓	7	8	9	10	11	12	▓	12	11	10	9	8	7	▓	7	8	9	10	11	12	▓	12	11	10	9	8	7	▓	5	4	3	2
▓	2	3	4	5	▓	7	8	9	10	11	12	11	10	9	8	7	▓	5	▓	7	8	9	10	11	12	11	10	9	8	7	▓	5	4	3	2	▓
12	▓	2	3	4	5	▓	7	8	9	10	11	10	9	8	7	▓	5	4	5	▓	7	8	9	10	11	10	9	8	7	▓	5	4	3	2	▓	12
11	12	▓	2	3	4	5	▓	7	8	9	10	11	10	9	8	7	▓	5	4	3	4	5	▓	7	8	9	10	11	10	9	8	7	▓	5	4	3	2	▓	12	11
10	11	12	▓	2	3	4	5	▓	7	8	9	8	7	▓	5	4	3	2	3	4	5	▓	7	8	9	8	7	▓	5	4	3	2	▓	12	11	10

Queen Size Extra Top Variation

|- - - -A- - - - -|B   C   D   E   D   C   B|- - - A - - -|B   C   D   E   D   C   B|- - - - - A - - - -|

1 2 3 4 5 6 7 8 9 10 11 12 13   14   15   16   17   18 19 20 21 22 23 24 25 26 27   28   29   30   31   32   33 34 35 36 37 38 39 40 41 42 43 44 45

3	4	5	▓	7	8	9	10	11	12	▓	2	3	4	5	▓	5	4	3	2	▓	12	11	2	3	4	5	▓	5	4	3	2	▓	12	11	10	9	8	7	▓	5	4	3
2	3	4	5	▓	7	8	9	10	11	12	▓	2	3	4	5	4	3	2	▓	12	11	10	11	12	▓	2	3	4	5	4	3	2	▓	12	11	10	9	8	7	▓	5	4	3	2
▓	2	3	4	5	▓	7	8	9	10	11	12	▓	2	3	4	3	2	▓	12	11	10	9	10	11	12	▓	2	3	4	3	2	▓	12	11	10	9	8	7	▓	5	4	3	2
12	▓	2	3	4	5	▓	7	8	9	10	11	12	▓	2	3	2	▓	12	11	10	9	8	9	10	11	12	▓	2	3	2	▓	12	11	10	9	8	7	▓	5	4	3	2	▓
11	12	▓	2	3	4	5	▓	7	8	9	10	11	12	▓	2	▓	12	11	10	9	8	7	8	9	10	11	12	▓	2	▓	12	11	10	9	8	7	▓	5	4	3	2	▓	12	11
10	11	12	▓	2	3	4	5	▓	7	8	9	10	11	12	▓	12	11	10	9	8	7	▓	7	8	9	10	11	12	▓	12	11	10	9	8	7	▓	5	4	3	2	▓	12	11	10
9	10	11	12	▓	2	3	4	5	▓	7	8	9	10	11	12	11	10	9	8	7	▓	5	▓	7	8	9	10	11	12	11	10	9	8	7	▓	5	4	3	2	▓	12	11	10	9
8	9	10	11	12	▓	2	3	4	5	▓	7	8	9	10	11	10	9	8	7	▓	5	4	5	▓	7	8	9	10	11	10	9	8	7	▓	5	4	3	2	▓	12	11	10	9	8
7	8	9	10	11	12	▓	2	3	4	5	▓	7	8	9	10	9	8	7	▓	5	4	3	4	5	▓	7	8	9	10	9	8	7	▓	5	4	3	2	▓	12	11	10	9	8	7
▓	7	8	9	10	11	12	▓	2	3	4	5	▓	7	8	9	8	7	▓	5	4	3	2	3	4	5	▓	7	8	9	8	7	▓	5	4	3	2	▓	12	11	10	9	8	7

COLOR VALUE VARIATIONS

Hint

Make copies of the Blank Layout Plan on page 17 and have fun experimenting with color value placements.

The following are examples of how changing the color value run alters the look of the heart design. The boxes below each illustration represent the numbered fabric swatches, and show how each effect was achieved.

Example 1

This arrangement, shading from light to dark/dark to light, is the reverse of the standard arrangement shown on page 15. The same fabrics have been used, but the color family value runs have been arranged in reverse order. This arrangement results in a dark center heart area, whereas the standard arrangement has a light center. Note that in this example, a fabric from Color Family 2 is in the #1 position. This is done so that the colors blend smoothly into the center of the heart.

Example 1 Light to Dark, Dark to Light

Color Family 1

Color Family 2

Examples 2 and 3

To keep a smooth color flow in these two examples, one of the color families has 7 fabrics and the other has 5. The difference in appearance results from how the color values of each family are arranged. In Example 2, the values shade from dark to light/dark to light. In Example 3, the two color families shade from light to dark/light to dark.

Example 2 Dark to Light, Dark to Light

Color Family 1

1 2 3 4 5 6 7 8 9 10 11 12

Color Family 2

Example 3 Light to Dark, Light to Dark

Color Family 1

1 2 3 4 5 6 7 8 9 10 11 12

Color Family 2

11

Borders

I recommend adding borders to provide a frame for the Bargello Heart top and to enlarge most of the tops to standard bed sizes. They also provide a "drop," the fabric that hangs over the sides of a bed to cover the mattress. One or more borders, cut in varying widths, are used to accomplish this.

I like to frame my Bargello Heart Quilts with three borders (except for the Mini and the Baby quilt sizes), each one a different fabric. Using a featured fabric twice, alternating it with a second fabric, is an attractive variation. There are many color photographs in the "Bargello Heart Gallery" (pages 33–48) to help inspire design ideas for your borders.

The chart on the following page lists the border widths to cut for each size quilt top. If you choose to alter the widths of the borders, remember to buy the appropriate yardage.

Determining Border Lengths (Sides)

Quilts, especially wall hangings, look their best when they lie flat. A quilt that ripples usually has borders that are not the same length. The parallel sides of a quilt top must each be made to fit the same length border strips. To determine the correct length, lay the quilt top on a flat surface and measure each of the sides and down the center. These measurements should be the same. If there is a difference, take the average of the measurements and cut two side border strips this length.

Assembly (Sides)

I cut my border strips from selvage edge to selvage edge and piece them together. Cut off the woven selvages before joining the strips together to get the correct length.

Center one border along one of the side edges. Pin the border to the top at the center and at each end. In some cases it might be necessary to ease in or gently stretch the side to fit. Use ¼" seam allowances to sew the border on. Press the seam allowances toward the border. Sew the other side border onto the quilt in the same manner.

Top and Bottom Borders

Repeat the process for the top and bottom edges. Measure the full width of the quilt along the top and bottom edges, including the border widths just added. If the measurements are not the same, again take the average of the measurements to determine the length of the top and bottom borders. Create two border pieces this length. Pin the border strips in place, making the edges fit, and sew using a ¼" seam allowance. Press the seam allowances toward the border.

Attach additional borders in the same fashion. Sew parallel sides, first one and then the other, and press the seam allowances toward the new border fabric.

Border Widths

	First Border	Second Border	Third Border
Mini Size Quilt	1½"	3½"	—
Baby Size Quilt	5"	—	—
Basic Size Quilt	2½"	3½"	6"
Twin Size Quilt	2½"	3½"	6"
Full Size Quilt	2½"	3½"	6"
Queen Size Quilt	2½"	3½"	6"
King Size Quilt	3"	5"	7"

12
Finishing

Now that the quilt top is complete, it can be layered with the batting and backing layers, and then basted together. Either machine or hand quilting can be done, or the top can be tied. Complex quilting designs should be marked on the top before the quilt layers are stacked and basted together. After the quilting is completed, binding is added and the quilt is ready for use.

Muslin is an excellent backing fabric choice. It is available in white, natural, black, and a limited number of colors. It comes in standard fabric widths (44") and wider widths (90" and 108").

I do not recommend using a sheet for a backing, as sheets have more threads per square inch than calico or muslin. This can cause the back to behave differently from the fabrics in your quilt top. Also, a sheet is difficult to hand quilt through.

The Backing Layer

The backing is the first layer of the basting "sandwich." Using standard width fabric for the backing will require piecing for the larger quilts. (Backing yardage is listed in the Supply List, on page 8.)

To determine the size of the backing piece, first measure the length and width of the finished quilt top. Add a *minimum* of 4" to both the width and length measurements. The additional inches allow for fabric shifting during the basting and/or quilting process. Depending on the width and length of the quilt top, the fabric for the backing can be seamed vertically or horizontally.

Figure 36 shows the different layouts that can be used to piece the backing. Determine which piecing layout works best for the quilt size you have made. Cut the required lengths for your layout. Remove the selvages and join the fabric lengths together with a ¼" seam. Removing the selvage prevents the seam(s) from puckering. Press both seam allowances to one side, making sure to press out any folds or creases.

The Batting Layer

The batting needs to be as large, or a bit larger, than the backing fabric. Use the measurements of the backing to purchase a batt large enough for your quilt. Batts can be purchased either in prepackaged sizes or by the yard.

Figure 36 Assembling the backing

Horizontally pieced backing

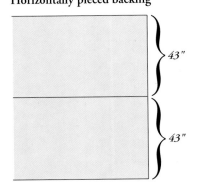

Accommodates a quilt top up to 85" long and any width

Vertically pieced backing

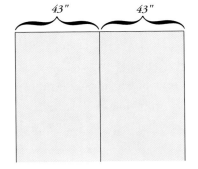

Accommodates a quilt top up to 85" wide and any length

Vertically pieced backing

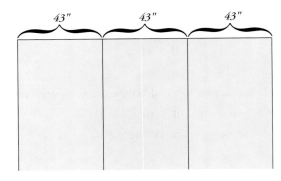

Accommodates a quilt top up to 126" wide and any length

The Quilt Top Layer

Before starting the layering process, take the time to give the quilt top one last pressing. Now is the time to remove any wrinkles and creases.

Complex quilt designs need to be marked before the three layers (top, batt, and backing) are basted together. Do not overlook marking the borders at this time. Marking is not necessary if you plan to quilt "in the ditch" or in diagonal lines "by eye." (See page 94 for illustrations of these two methods.)

To determine how far apart the quilting design lines should be, read the recommended quilting requirements on your batt packaging. Batts that are 100% cotton require quilting that is no farther apart than 1". Some cotton/polyester blends and 100% polyester batts can be quilted up to 6" apart. The distances vary because of the fiber content and the manufacturing process. Follow the quilting guidelines for the type of batt you choose to ensure that the batting does not tear apart with use or lump up when washed.

> ### Hint
>
> *For pin basting, put safety pins in without closing them until they are all in place. This keeps the layers from shifting each time the quilt is lifted to close a pin. If all the pins are in place the layers do not shift as the pins are closed. Try to avoid placing pins on quilting lines. This way few pins will need to be moved while quilting.*
>
> *The pins should be no farther apart than 4". The more pins you use, the less chance there is of the layers shifting, which would cause puckers while quilting. A queen size quilt needs approximately 450 pins.*

LAYERING AND BASTING

Spread the backing fabric, right side down, on a flat, clean surface. Anchor it down with pins or masking tape. This keeps the backing from slipping and bunching as the other layers are placed over it.

Next spread the batting over the backing and gently smooth out any wrinkles.

The top is then centered, right side up, over the batting. Take care not to stretch the top. Gently smooth the top out from the center to the edges.

Basting holds the layers of the quilt together temporarily as they are quilted. The layers can be basted together by hand with large basting stitches, or pin basted with safety pins. (Do not use straight pins, they will scratch your hands badly during quilting. I know from experience.) To hold the three layers together I prefer pin basting with size 1 safety pins. Larger safety pins leave big holes and smaller pins are difficult to handle.

Start basting from the center and work out to the edges. Do a row of basting horizontally, starting from the center, to each side edge. Then do a basting row vertically to the top and bottom edges. Next, diagonal rows of basting are sewn, from the center, out to each corner. To finish basting, sew rows in a grid pattern about 3" to 4" apart, horizontally and vertically, over the whole top (Figure 37).

Figure 37 Stitched basting

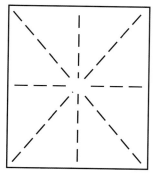

First, baste from the center outwards

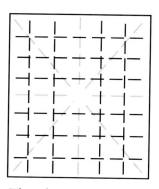

Then, baste in a grid pattern

Figure 38 Quilting diagonally "by eye"

QUILTING

The Bargello Heart design area, with all its seams, may be difficult to hand quilt. After hand quilting her own Baby size quilt, my friend, Billie Perry, who *likes* to do hand quilting, requested that I machine quilt her Queen size quilt. So hand quilting can be done but…be prepared to use a lot of strength, patience, and pliers!

Most of the quilts featured in this book are quilted "by eye" diagonally through every other row (Figure 38). Several others are quilted "in the ditch," skipping two or three rows in both directions (Figure 39). Since there is no marking necessary in the heart area, these two methods, "by eye" and "in the ditch," can be quilted quickly.

If you machine quilt, use a walking foot, also known as an even feed foot or quilting foot. This special foot feeds the layers of the quilt evenly under the needle to help eliminate puckers.

Figure 39 Quilting "in the ditch"

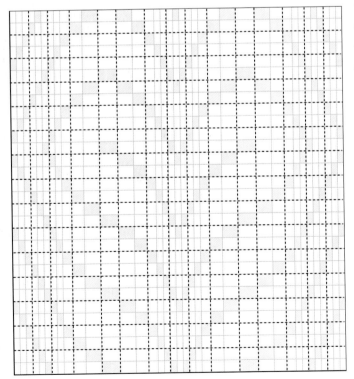

BINDING

The final step to complete the quilt is finishing the edges. Use your preferred method of binding or edge treatment. There are numerous publications that have helpful and clear instructions on finishing quilts.

Yardage for the binding is given on page 8 in the "Supply List." The amount listed is enough fabric for a double layered binding, that is then folded over to the back side and finished either by machine or hand.

There are many books available that cover finishing, quilting, and binding procedures in detail. See "Suggested Reading" on page 95 for a selection of books that I have found informative.